Andrea Seilheimer

Human Resource Accounting

Suitable methods for assessing human resources in the civil service

Andrea Seilheimer

HUMAN RESOURCE ACCOUNTING

Suitable methods for assessing human resources in the civil service

ibidem-Verlag
Stuttgart

Bibliografische Information der Deutschen Nationalbibliothek
Die Deutsche Nationalbibliothek verzeichnet diese Publikation in der Deutschen Nationalbibliografie; detaillierte bibliografische Daten sind im Internet über http://dnb.d-nb.de abrufbar.

Bibliographic information published by the Deutsche Nationalbibliothek
Die Deutsche Nationalbibliothek lists this publication in the Deutsche Nationalbibliografie; detailed bibliographic data are available in the Internet at http://dnb.d-nb.de.

Coverbild: © Gerd Altmann / PIXELIO

∞

Gedruckt auf alterungsbeständigem, säurefreien Papier
Printed on acid-free paper

ISBN-13: 978-3-8382-0434-5

© *ibidem*-Verlag
Stuttgart 2012

Printed in Germany

Preliminary note

This book was first published in German in 2007. It focused both on the situation and changes of Human Resource Accounting in the German state of Hesse at the beginning of this decade. Meanwhile, things have developed, and there have been many changes in the areas of budget, public finances, civil service career law, public services law, and concerning projects. For this reason, it seemed to me that it was time now to work this book over in order to take account for those changes that might have an influence on the subject of this book. What is more, I wanted to open it for the English-speaking world, and so I decided to translate it into English. The present second edition is the result of this work.

To make this new edition possible, I would like to thank Rita Reiter-Mollenhauer, Hessian Ministry for Social Affairs, Karl-Wilhelm Schmidt and Volkmar Drachsler, both Hessian Ministry of the Interior and Sports, Mrs. Raubach, Sigrid Balsys, and Dr. Peter Buck, Statistical Office of Hesse. I would also thank Clare Meuren and Claudia Thierolf for their respective support. Thanks to Prof. Dr. Wolfgang Beiersdorf, Hochschule Darmstadt, who made me familiar with Human Resource Accounting a long time ago. Thanks again to ibidem for their trust in me, especially to Valerie Lange, who made it possible to put this publication into practice.

Furthermore, I would like to thank all those people who estimate me for my love for languages, my abilities, the meticulous way I work, and just for the way how I am. Thanks again to my family, who knows me being busy such a lot of time at my desk. Thanks to God who always supports me in what I do.

August 2012   Andrea Seilheimer

II. Table of Abbreviations

BDSG	Federal Data Protection Act (Ger. 'Bundesdatenschutzgesetz')
BGBl	Federal Law Gazette (Ger. 'Bundesgesetzblatt')
BPersVG	Federal Law on Employee Representation (Ger. 'Bundespersonalvertretungsgesetz')
bzw.	beziehungsweise (Engl. 'respectively', 'or rather')
c.	cipher LAW (Ger. 'Ziffer')
cf.	compare further
cl.	clause LAW (Ger. 'Satz')
e.g.	for example (Lat. exempli gratia)
et al.	and others, mostly for authors (Lat. 'et alteri')
etc.	and others, mostly for items (Lat. 'et cetera')
f/ff	and the following page/s
Ger.	German
GG	Basic Law for the Federal Republic of Germany [Ger. 'Grundgesetz')
GVBl	Journal of Laws and Ordinances (Ger. 'Gesetz- und Verordnungsblatt')
HDSG	Hessian Data Protection Act (Ger. 'Hessisches Datenschutzgesetz')
HPVG	Hessian Law on Employee Representation (Ger. 'Hessisches Personalvertretungsgesetz')
HR	Human Resources
HRA	Human Resource Accounting
i.e.	that is; this means (Lat. 'id est')
IFRS	International Financial Reporting Standards
Illustr.	illustration
Lat.	Latin
LHO	Hessian Budget Provisions (Ger. 'Hessische Landeshaushaltsordnung')
n.d.	not dated
p.	page
par.	paragraph LAW (Ger. 'Absatz')
RGBl	National Gazette (Ger. 'Reichsgesetzblatt')
s./ss.	section/s LAW (Ger. 'Paragraph')
Tab.	table
TVöD	Collective Agreement for Public Employees (Ger. 'Tarifvertrag für den öffentlichen Dienst')

US/USA/U.S.A.	United States/United States of America
US-GAAP	United States Generally Accepted Accounting Principles
W.A.	without author
w.y.	without year

III. Table of Illustrations

IV. List of Tables

For God and my parents.

Abstract

In this work, after defining both "human resources" and "Human Resource Accounting", and treating the origins and the distribution of this area of research, various operational in- and output-oriented methods of Human Resource Accounting were presented at first. In a second step, the application of these methods in the civil service was examined in detail. Furthermore, the legal framework and the general prerequisites for a Human Resource Accounting system in the civil service were outlined. Finally, structural recommendations on the implementation of such a system rounded this work off.

Zusammenfassung

In dieser Arbeit wurden zunächst die Begriffe "human resources" und "Human Resource Accounting" definiert sowie Ursprung und Verbreitung dieses Forschungsgebiets dargestellt, bevor auf betriebswirtschaftliche in- und outputorientierte Methoden der Humanvermögensrechnung eingegangen wurde. In einem weiteren Schritt erfolgte eine detaillierte Analyse zur Anwendung dieser Methoden im öffentlichen Dienst. Darüber hinaus wurden die rechtlichen Rahmenbedingungen für und die allgemeinen Anforderungen an ein Human Resource Accounting-System im öffentlichen Dienst herausgestellt. Schließlich rundeten strukturelle Empfehlungen zur Implementierung eines solchen Systems dieses Buch ab.

1. The difficulty to assess human resources in the civil service[1]

"The money has run out". The Federal Republic of Germany, the German laender and municipalities are seeing themselves confronted with acute financial distress at the moment. Budget deficits, an increasing absolute level of national debt, and the introduction of a "debt brake" usually cut back the government's financial flexibility more and more. In the past, financial resources dedicated both to material and human resources were cut regularly not only to reduce public total expenditures, but also to contain the high level of public debt. In order to reach these aims, there have primarily been a lower number of employments in the public service since the beginning of the nineties of the 20th century. What is more, vacancies frequently haven't been refilled, and promotions have been conducted in a more restricted way to reduce the high proportion of personnel costs of the overall public expenses. In the same period of time, a constant increase of public tasks could be registered in the civil service due to changes in society, the progressing Europeanization, and a modified information technology. For a person who works in the public service, this means to be confronted both with a greater variety of tasks and with increasing demands of employers – yet without getting a higher remuneration for this. Even if the factor "personnel" plays an important role for task fulfillment in the public service, the value of public employees is not recorded anywhere, nor are they considered as "assets", but merely as an item of expenditure in the budget of their authorities. The consequence of this is that neither the "value" of single employees nor the overall HR value at the disposal of authorities is known; therefore, it cannot be used for decision making in the various activity fields of the public sector. For this reason, inefficient decisions do not only lead to high costs, but also increase public expenses, and therefore contribute to the further increase of national debt.

One solution for these problems would be the use of suitable methods of Human Resource Accounting in the civil service: With the aid of these methods, the

---

[1] In this work, both the terms "Public Service" and "Civil Service", and "state administration" and "public administration" are used as synonyms.

"value" of human resources could be identified and used purpose-specifically in many areas of efficient decision-making in the public sector. This in turn would lead to cost savings, the long-term decrease in public expenses as well as the reduction of the high level of public debt.

The aim of this work is to examine which Human Resource Accounting methods would be suitable for the civil service. For this purpose, the following thread will be a guideline for this work: At first, the notions "human resources" and "Human Resource Accounting" will be defined. Furthermore, the origins and the distribution of Human Resource Accounting will be illustrated. In the next step, current Human Resource Accounting method will be presented in a general way. After the analysis of the current situation of Human Resource Accounting in the Hessian state administration and of Hesse's requirements in the area of Human Resource Accounting, general requirements for a Human Resource Accounting system, and special demands of stakeholder groups will be worked out. In a further step, from the gap between the current situation and Hesse's requirements in this field, the main purposes of a Human Resource Accounting system will be deduced for the public sector. After this, the analysis of suitable Human Resource Accounting methods for the public sector will be the focal point of interest, before the framework conditions and the requirements for an implementation of such methods in the civil service will be discussed. After all, structural recommendations for a Human Resource Accounting system will round off this work.

2. Human Resource Accounting

Current accounting systems are based upon the assumption that employees are an expense item (cf. Hekimian/Jones 1967, 106): Only under the aspect of "wages and salaries" are people recorded in the ordinary profit and loss account. However, because of the tertiarization process of the global economy, the service factor becomes more and more important in this world. One consequence of this is that – despite the high stage both of technical and computer-based developments – human resources haven't yet stopped to become "the" crucial production factor in companies, and thus, they have an outstanding meaning for the companies' performance. From this, we can draw the conclusion that it could be useful to consider and evaluate employees as valuable company resources or as "assets", and to transfer both analytical and conceptual assessment approaches of the management of tangibles or financial assets to the management of human resources (cf. Hekimian/Jones 1967, 111).

2.1 Definition of "Human Resources" and "Human Resource Accounting"

There exists no standard definition of *"human resources"* in scientific papers; this notion is rather used in different ways (cf. Gebauer/Wall 2002, 685). Furthermore, synonyms like "human capital", "human potential", "human resources" and "human assets" are current:

Schultz (cf. Schultz 1971, 1-17)	*Human capital* ("Humankapital") is all the knowledge and all the skills of a certain group of people or of one single person with economic value
Bösch (cf. Bösch 1979, 34)	*Human resources* (*"Humanvermögen"*) is the target achievement that can be expected and made available from the employees' and from the firm's achievement potential
Aschoff (cf. Aschoff 1978, 4ff)	*Operational human capital* (*"Betriebliches Humankapital bzw. Humanvermögen"*) is the amount of contracted employees' performance potential at the disposal of a company.
Beyer (cf. Beyer 1991, 162)	*Human resources* (*"Humanvermögen"*) is the amount of all costs for acquisition, preservation, long-term use of the employee (=investment in the person).
Fischer (cf. Fischer 1999, 33)	*Human potential* are the demands of a company towards the employees' future supply of a certain kind, amount and quality

	of achievement potential, and which can be *expected* to be available for the firm in future
OECD (1996, 22, cited after Frederiksen/Westphalen 1998, 20)	"In general [sic] *human capital* can be defined as the knowledge that individuals acquire during their lifetimes and use to produce goods, services or ideas in market or non-market circumstances"

Illustr. 1: Definitions and synonyms for "human resources"

Apart from these definitions, there are bordering notions which are partly attributed to human capital, but partly go beyond it as for example "knowledge capital", "intellectual capital", "intangibles" or "structural capital" (cf. Gebauer/Wall 2002, 685/686). In German literature, the notion "human capital" is used as an equivalent for the Anglo-Saxon term "human capital" ("human assets", "human resources") (cf. Aschoff 1978, 4ff). As there is a large number of very distinct content-related definitions for human resources, the definition of Beyer, according to whom human resources are considered as the amount of costs for the acquisition, the preservation and the long-term use of a company's employees (=investment in the person), is taken as a basis in this work. By evaluating past, present or future costs of a firm's human resources, the difficult task of quantifying personnel-related data can probably be rendered possible.

The notion *"Human Resource Accounting"* (HRA)[2] stands for attempts to quantify "employee values" for companies, as this value is considered to be the crucial factor of production (cf. Beyer 1991, 161). Terms like "Personalvermögensrech-nung", "Humankapitalrechnung", "Humanpotentialrech-nung" and others are used as synonyms in German speaking countries (cf. Fischer 1999, 39). From the operational point of view, the Anglo-Saxon terms "Human Resource Accounting" (HRA) and the German one "Humanvermögensrechnung" are most commonly used. The notion "Human Resource Accounting" in its actual application was introduced in 1968 in the Anglo-Saxon area; there, it was defined as

> [...] the process of identifying, measuring, and communicating information about human resources to facilitate effective management within an organization (Brummet et al. 1968, 20).

However, there are still more definitions, boundaries, and functions of "Human Resource Accounting", as can be seen in the following table (cf. Maier 1980, 13f):

---

[2] In Germany, the term *"Humanvermögensrechnung"* is common.

Human Resource Accounting as ...
1. ... the analogous capital budgeting of a business' human resources and tangible assets: Attempts to quantify investments in a company's staff to have better bases for decision-making (Human resources as an investment asset)
2. ... *a subsidiary tool* to gather both costs and benefits of a business' human resources (cost-benefit-analysis)
3. ... *a statement for annual accounts:* Instrument to illustrate operational human resources in internal and/or external company reports (balance sheets, profit and loss reports etc.)
4. ... *staff and management information system:* Tool to identify, gather, process information on operational human assets in order to optimize the management

Illustr. 2: Definitions and functions of "Human Resource Accounting"

There are even more definitions of Human Resource Accounting:

> HRA can be considered both an internal and an external discipline: internal as a management tool; external as a reporting tool. In HRA, human resources are viewed as assets or investments of the organisation [sic] (Frederiksen/Westphalen 1998, 17).

> HRA was originally defined as the process of identifying, measuring, and communicating information about human resources to facilitate management within an organisation [sic]. It is an extension of the accounting principles of matching costs and revenues and of organising [sic] data to communicate relevant information in financial terms. However, the process includes the concept of accounting for the condition of human capabilities and their value as provided by the measurement tools of the behavioural [sic] sciences (Philips, J. (1996, 36, cited after Frederiksen/Westphalen 1998, 17-18).

According to Sackmann et al. (1989), the objective of Human Resource Accounting is to quantify the economic value of people for organizations to have input information for management and financial decisions (cf. Armstrong 2001, 58).

2.2 Origins and distribution of Human Resource Accounting

From the historical point of view, macroeconomic and microeconomic assessment approaches for human resources must be distinguished.

On the *macroeconomic level*, there were early and repeated attempts to record the value both of individuals and of all members of a national economy. The "evaluation" of a person for determined purposes goes back to the times of prehistoric slave trade and was of regional importance up to and including the 19th

21

century (cf. Schoenfeld 1974, 1). Picking up Babylonian concepts, there were also human accounting valuation methods for other purposes in Germanic Law. For instance, there was a determined asset valuation for slain people to enable the provision of damages (cf. Woods/Metzger 1927, 64). Macroeconomic approaches for the assessment of human resources build up on the same bases (cf. Schoenfeld 1974, 2). According to them, accounting human resources depends on the following factors:

- ... costs for the "production" and "maintenance" of a human being (nutrition, education, accommodation etc.) (Adam Smith)
- ... contribution to the national product (Sir William Petty); Petty tried to calculate the value of Great Britain's human capital (cf. Gebauer/Wall 2002, 686)
- ... future earnings (as a manifestation of the contribution to the national product), less the maintenance costs (Sir Robert Giffen)

However, all macroeconomic HRA approaches were contradicted often. As the value of each individual person obviously cannot be determined by one single formula, and because of the difficulty of the measurement, many suggestions have been made to abstain from such calculations; nevertheless, it seems possible to approximately assess the value of a bigger amount of people for a strictly defined purpose (e.g. the measurement of educational investment) (cf. Schoenfeld 1974, 2-3). In this work, though, macroeconomic Human Resource Accounting approaches are left aside, as suitable assessment methods for the civil service, notably in the German state Hesse, are the focal point of interest.

On the *microeconomic level*, in the twenties of the last century, it was discussed whether the use of tangible assets without the production factor "human productive capacity" was impossible (cf. Paton 1922, 486, and Nicklisch 1932 – but also in former editions already). Some decades later, Human Resource Accounting had its roots in the middle of the sixties of the past century. In those days, it should serve to regularly and systematically gather information on monetary and behavior-related aspects of human resources; thus, it could be used directly for problematic areas of decision-making by the business management (cf. Fischer-

Winkelmann/Hohl 1982, 125 and 128). In this context, the determination of the future monetary value of operational human capital mostly was the main focus (cf. Fischer 1999, 39-40). Although it was impossible to find articles on Human Resource Accounting in Europe at the beginning of the seventies, about 30 works had already been published in the USA and Canada at that time; after all, at the beginning of 1972, the first French papers appeared (cf. Marquès 1982, 227). At the same time, the first English contributions emerged in this area, and in 1972, the first publications came up in Switzerland; then, in 1973, after several international seminars had taken place, this was also the case in Germany. The most intense phase of drafts and developments of Human Resource Accounting theories was between the end of the sixties and the beginning of the eighties of the 20th century - with works of Flamholtz, Likert, Jaggi, Lau, Conrads, Aschoff and others (cf., e.g., Fischer-Winkelmann/Hohl 1982 as an overall view) (cf. Fischer 1999, 39). Until the middle of the seventies of the last century, several human capital concepts were implemented in a series of companies (cf. Gebauer/Wall 2002, 686). The first US-company to apply the concept of Human Resource Accounting in practice was the R.G. Barry Corporation of Columbus, Ohio, in 1968. The Barry Corporation, located in the footwear industry, had 3,000 employees in six US states in 1972 (cf. Neubauer 1974, 266). There, Human Resource Accounting was initially practiced for 96 managers only, and until 1972, it was extended to about 1,200 employees (cf. Maier 1990, 27). Even though at first, research efforts were vehemently pressed ahead with great expectations, the meaning of Human Resource Accounting as an independent line of research has decreased continually since the end of the seventies (cf. Streim 1993, 1692). Due to apparently insurmountable problems with data provision and handling, only a few specialists were able to establish appropriate accounting systems (cf. Gebauer/Wall 2002, 686).

One of the biggest problems which have led to the stagnation of Human Resource Accounting are the mostly insufficiently defined or partly even not at all described purposes of accounting objectives and application situations of HRA methods[3]. A few works (as the one of Conrads et al. 1982), containing very specific targets and measurement methods, instruments, and conditions to calculate the value of human

---

[3] On the general review of Human Resource Accounting cf. Fischer-Winkelmann/Hohl 1982;
    Kontner 1980, 52-102 and 113f; Schoenfeld 1974; Winckler 1991, 173; Dawson 1988, 31;
    Eichenberger 1992, 208-215.

resources and its respective transformations, are only an adequate solution for specific decision-making situations with exactly defined operations and certain target functions (cf. Fischer 1999, 40).

However, there are still more problems which have led to the stagnation of Human Resource Accounting. These are the following ones (cf. Fischer 1999, 40f):

Kind of problems	Description
instrumental problems	• All methods to evaluate the earning power either fail because of attributive problems and/or do not meet minimum requirements of objectivity, reliability, and validity.
normative problems	• possibility of work council participation according to the code of industrial relations • provisions of the Federal Data Protection Act ("Bundesdatenschutzgesetz")
moral/ethical problems	• moral/ethical restrictions of research perspectives such as considering people as financial assets or as "property" of the company (cf. Armstrong 2001, 58)
acceptance problems	• among employees and managers (most notably if the introduction of a Human Resource Accounting system contradicts the postulated business principles and/or if it does not comply with the existing corporate culture)
other problems	• difficulty or impossibility to give detailed information on measurement and assessment methods to be used for the self-declared research targets, but which are independent of concrete conditions and objective functions, if different approaches and various instruments are necessary for the assessment

Illustr. 3: Reasons for the stagnation of Human Resource Accounting

The *holistic concept* of Human Resource Accounting should step aside the traditional accounting system or augment it remarkably, but it has hence become scientifically meaningless and practically irrelevant (cf. Fischer 1999, 40). It was replaced by a *partially purpose-oriented* valuation with regard to special aspects of human resources: To some extent, HRA-approaches are integrated in single areas of personnel planning such as selection procedures in recruitment planning (cf. Gerpott 1990, 37-44), profile methods for the comparison of requirements and aptitudes during the employment planning process, learning curve concepts during the formation planning, or calculations on fluctuation costs (cf. Streim 1982, 130-146). The interest in Human Resource Accounting approaches was reawaken only because of to two different facts in the nineties of the twentieth century: On the one hand, US-American companies saw themselves confronted with a growing competition pressure from large-scale Japanese enterprises: Advantages in productivity were traced back to the consequent maintenance of human resources – this was a contrast to the American "hire and fire-philosophy" (cf. Gebauer/Wall 2002, 686). On the other hand, the service sector became more and more important: This is the reason why in the New Economy of the nineties, an increasing amount of asset positions evolved in the book value. This, in turn, caused a visibly growing gap between the market value and the book value of many companies (cf. Gebauer/Wall 2002, 686, and Deutsch 1997, 3):

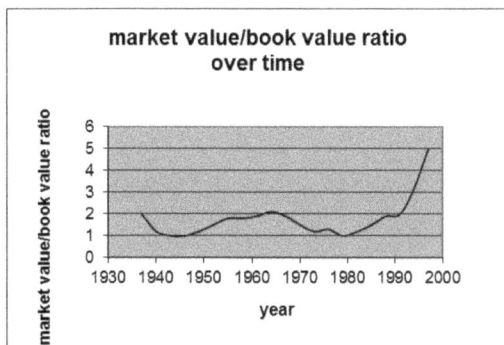

market value/book value ratio over time

market value/book value ratio

6
5
4
3
2
1
0

1930 1940 1950 1960 1970 1980 1990 2000

year

Illustr. 4: Market value/book value over time

The "book value" or rather the "residual value" is defined as those parts of the assets or debit items of a commercial business' balance sheet which are assessed according to the acquisition costs or the manufacturing costs, and corrected according to depreciation and write-ups pursuant to commercial and tax law (cf. Gabler Wirtschaftslexikon 1993, 601). The market value is also defined as the current or daily value or price for a good traded at the market at a certain time (cf. Gabler Wirtschaftslexikon 1993, 2215 and 3226f). While for the assessment of book value positions, only reported items are allowed to be taken into account, the assessment of a company's market value also requires considering "items" which cannot be recorded in the balance sheet or which actually differ in value from the recorded book-keeping value. This is often the case with patents, licenses, the "research and development" sector, and an existing goodwill (cf. Frederiksen/Westphalen 1998, 25). Besides, a company's human resources also represent an intangible asset; they are not a part of the book value, but have substantial influence on the market value. Therefore, the gap between market and book values of companies could be explained by means of suitable methods of Human Resource Accounting (cf. Gebauer/Wall 2002, 686).

3. Methods of Human Resource Accounting

Almost at the same time, many authors have already focused on the subject of "Human Resource Accounting". Over time, this led to the development of different ways of classification of Human Resource Accounting methods. Below, three different ways of structuring Human Resource Accounting models will be presented.

Gebauer and Wall (cf. 2002, 686-687, and Gebauer 2002, 83) classify the multitude of the up to now developed Human Resource Accounting methods on the basis of two characteristics (cf. illustr. 5):

1. on the basis of the *valuation object*: "individals" vs. "homogeneous groups of persons " or
2. on the basis of the *resulting dimension*: "monetary" vs. "non-monetary" information on human resources.

Accounting models for human resources

object: individuals

monetary | non-monetary

non-monetary (individuals):
- individual and typical organizational determinants of value after *Flamholtz*
- business capital after *Esselborn/Henke*

monetary (individuals):

cost based
- historical acquisition costs after *Brummet/Flamholtz/Pyle*
- replacement costs after *Flamholtz*
- opportunity costs after *Hekimian/Jones*
- future expenditures after *Lev/Schwartz*
- future adjusted discounted expenditures after *Hermanson*

value based
- future contribution to performance without hierarchy levels after *Waters*
- future contribution to performance with hierarchy levels after *Flamholtz*

object: groups

monetary | non-monetary

non-monetary (groups):
- individual and collective variables of behavior after *Likert*
- individual variables of behavior after *Myers/Flowers*
- Human Capital Index after *Pfau*

monetary (groups):

cost based
- historical acquisition costs after *Pyle*
- replacement costs after *Likert*
- future expenditures after *Lev/Schwartz*

value based
- historical business profits after *Hermanson*
- future business profits after *Brummet/Flamholtz/Pyle*
- future contribution to performance after *Jaggi/Lau*
- Skandia Navigator after *Edvinsson*

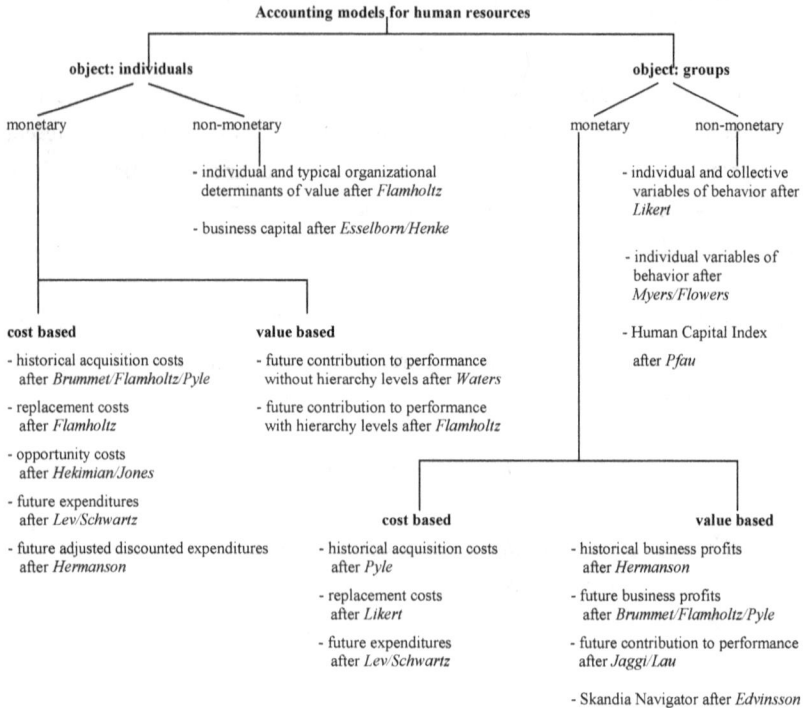

Illustr. 5: Overview of Human Resource Accounting methods

While statements of *monetary results* can be interpreted relatively easily, the application of *non-monetary methods* also requires having a close look at the respectively applied scales (cf. Gebauer/Wall 2002, 687).

Cost based methods make use of variables like costs, expenses, expenditures or human resource-related payments, whereas *value based* methods take up the benefits attributed to human capital as an assessment basis – i.e. the assessed future contributions to performance – (cf. Gebauer/Wall 2002, 687). *Value based* methods start out from the fact that assets cannot only be attributed to costs they rely on, but chiefly to anticipated future human performance contributions (cf. Gebauer/Wall 2002, 688).

Armstrong presents another division of Human Resource Accounting models (cf. Armstrong 2001, 58):

	Cost models	HR-value models	monetary models
Considering ...	historical costs, acquisition costs, replacement costs or opportunity costs	non-monetary behavior models and monetary-economic value models (combinations)	discounted estimations of future revenues

Illustr. 6: Types of Human Resource Accounting models

According to Flamholtz (cf. 1973, 82 ff.), input-oriented Human Resource Accounting methods only take into account negative success components such as staff expenditures like payments for remuneration, training, and further education etc.; yet, the so-called "output-oriented approaches" also consider positive success components (such as the benefits attributed to employees).

This chapter deals with a selection of the most important Human Resource Accounting methods. As Flamholtz' (1973) input-output-orientation of Human Resource Accounting methods appears to be well-arranged, and offers a good point of departure to outline the functionality of these methods, his way of describing the models is laid down as a basis for this work.

3.1 Input-oriented Human Resource Accounting Methods

For "input-oriented" Human Resource Accounting methods, past, present or future staff costs such as wages and salaries, replacement costs for an equivalent performance potential, or opportunity costs (i.e. values that allow an optimal allocation of given resources) are crucial for the HR assessment in a company (cf. Schoenfeld 1974, 9). In this section, the method of historical acquisition costs, the method of replacement costs, the method of opportunity costs, the adjusted discounted future wages model as well as the method of future earnings will be presented.

3.1.1 Historical Cost Method[4]

Assessing human resources on the basis of *historical costs* largely involves an equal treatment of expenditures for material and human resources (cf. Aschoff 1978, 15 ff.). Expenditures for human resources are also considered as investments, analogously to items of tangible assets that may take a significant influence on future revenues of companies.

The basis of the method of historical acquisition costs are the arising costs for human resources at a certain reference point (cf. Gebauer/Wall 2002, 687, and Schoenfeld 1974, 18). All personnel-related costs are registered functionally by types of costs and causing objects such as single employees and staff groups; they are divided into an asset and an expense component (cf. Beyer 1991, 162-163):

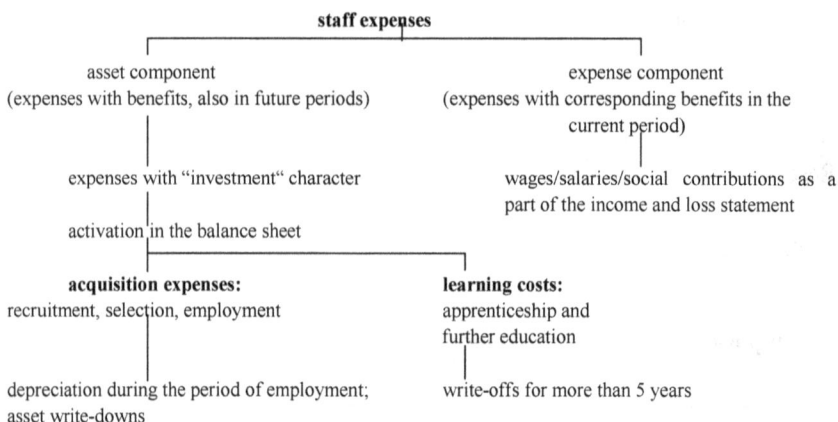

Illustr. 7: Structure of staff expenses (1)

This assessment method both considers direct and indirect costs, but makes a difference between *acquisition costs* and *learning costs* (cf. Flamholtz 2001, 59). Thus, all relevant costs are taken into account from recruitment and in-service

---

[4] The method is also called "Cost Benefit Method" or "Method of historical Acquisition Costs"; in the German language area, the HR-assessment method on the basis of historical costs is also called "Kostenwertmethode", "Methode der historischen Anschaffungskosten", and "Anschaffungskostenprinzip".

30

training to the decrease of productivity during the training phases (cf. Gebauer/Wall 2002, 688). All in all, historical acquisition costs comprise the following components (cf. Flamholtz 2001, 59):

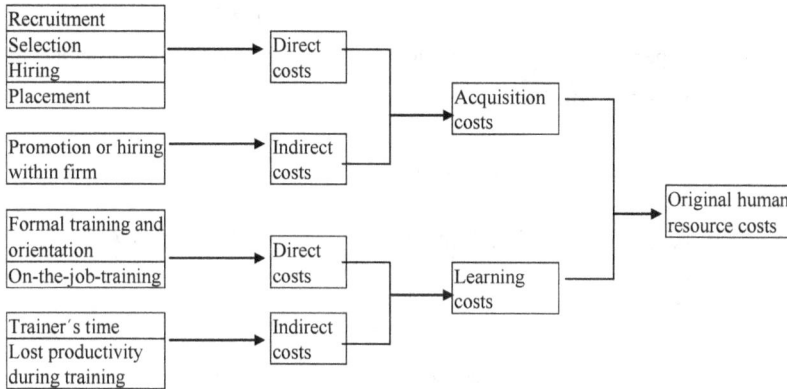

Illustr. 8: Overview of historical acquisition costs

The gathered costs are treated like investments in other operational sectors. Due to current consumption, extraordinary exhaustion or loss, they are subject to a constant decrease in value (cf. Schoenfeld 1974, 20). "Current consumption" can be described as the slow process of obsolescence of knowledge and skills etc., whereas "extraordinary exhaustion" or "loss" refers to those changes that completely eat up the asset component of each employee (cf. Schoenfeld 1974, 20f). Examples for this are dismissals as well as retirements due to health reasons. For the current consumption, different in-house consumption periods must be found out and adapted in a relatively short time. Schoenfeld (cf. 1974, 20) additionally weights the anticipated economic life with a probability factor, considering various influences such as the state of health, job satisfaction, remuneration, disturbing factors of the labor market, influences on the employee's private life etc. However, weighting the economic life under the cost value method is only mentioned in Schoenfeld's papers; therefore, the unweighted economic life will be laid down for HR assessment in the framework of the above mentioned method in this work.

This method has the aim to supply decision makers of the HR department with information on usual costs for staff acquisition or on investments in staff replacement at different hierarchy levels. What is more, information on human capital can serve as a basis for decision making for investments in human capital, too (cf. Gebauer/Wall 2002, 688). Furthermore, the cost value method does not only help make personnel decisions easier, but also control the performance of managers and register fluctuation (cf. Beyer 1991, 161-162).

The following example illustrates this method:

Type of expenditure or costs	Mr. Meier		Mrs. Schmidt	
	begin of period 1	end of period 1	begin of period 1	end of period 1
Costs for recruitment (in €) at the beginning of period 1 (investment character); anticipated balanced time remaining in the company (Mr. Meier: 5 years; Mrs. Müller: 10 years)	5,000,- % 1,000,- (depreciation)	4,000,-	2,000,- % 200,- (depreciation)	1,800,-
Expenditures for wages/ salaries p. a. (in €) in period 1 ("consumptive" expenditures)		30,000,-		10,000,-
Further education (useful life 3 years) at the beginning of period 1; depreciation 1/3 per annum ("investive expenditures")	3,000,-	2,000,-	9,000,-	6,000,-
Value of human assets at the end of period 1		**6,000,-**		**7,800,-**

Illustr. 9: Examples of an HR evaluation by means of the historical acquisition cost method

The assessment of human assets for more than one accounting period results in the value of human assets: This is the amount of all previous investments in human resources, less the ordinary and extraordinary depreciations. The creation of investment accounts does not only facilitate the evaluation of individual human assets, but also to get an overview of final inventories, notably of the change of original HR values. The following example shows the way of structuring personnel expenses according to Beyer (cf. 1991, 163).

Example:

investment account Müller			balance sheet	
Acquisition	45,000	Depreciation,	Fixed assets ...	Equity ...
Training	20,000	Further education	Current assets ...	Borrowed capital ...
Further education	20,000	(5 years) 4,000	Human assets ...	Human capital ...
		Depreciation, Expenditures for Acquisition (10 years) 6,500		
		Final stock 74,500		
	85,000	85,000		

Illustr. 10: Structure of personnel expenses (2)

The amount of an organization's human assets is represented in the asset side of the balance sheet. In contrast to this, "human capital" is recorded as a supplement of the items "equity" and "debts" in the liabilities side of the balance sheet.

The cost value method, though, holds the following problems (cf. Beyer 1991, 162f):

- determination of the useful life of investments in human resources, e.g. of training (deduction of the expected useful life from empirical values, or subjective estimations; depreciation on a straight-line basis over the determined period).
- determination of the useful life of recruitment investments: Useful life as an employee's expected remaining time in the company, with the maximum limit of "retirement age, less the actual age of the employee"; determinants: age, position, period of employment up to the reference point
- The actual state of obsolete training measures can only be gathered in special cases (by special depreciations).
- The gathered cost-related investments only represent an approximate amount for the value of human resources, as the educational background is not taken into account. Mincer (cf. 1962, 50ff) is of the opinion that about half of the amount of formation costs refer to the time before professional life begins, while operational formation and experience only represent a small part of the overall costs.

- The assumption of a causal connection between accumulated costs and rendered services shall be deemed to be critical.
- Expenditures on human resources are divided into an expense and an asset component.
- division into functional accounts
- division into personal-related accounts

Despite the problems of this assessment method, the cost value method was applied in several American companies (cf. Flamholtz 1973, 9 ff.). It is the most frequently used method of HR assessment, as it has the closest relationship with traditional accountancy (cf. Beyer 1991, 161). To sum it up, the method of historical acquisition costs represents a practicable way of assessing human assets.

3.1.2 Replacement Cost Method

Within the framework of the replacement cost method, employees are not assessed according to their acquisition costs, but rather to their replacement costs, i.e. to the costs that would accrue if they had to be replaced by a person with both an equivalent formation and experience (cf. Hekimian/Jones 1967, 107). As the recruitment of an organizational member of "the same quality" is almost impossible, only those acquisition costs can at best be taken into account which would incur for someone who would be able to fulfill the same tasks of the same quality, and in the same position like another organizational member ("positional replacement costs")[5] (cf. Aschoff 1978, 178, and Flamholtz 1973, 10ff.).

Given that inflationary trends are also taken into account, the replacement value of an organizational member is usually higher than the original acquisition value. This is shown in the following example:

Mr. Schulze's original acquisition and learning costs of € 15,000,- are accumulated up to a planned "replacement date" (t = 10). The accumulation factor is 3% p.a.:

$$€\ 15,000,- \times (1 + 3\%)^{10} = \underline{€\ 20,158.75}$$

---

[5] For this reason, Flamholtz (cf. 1973, 62 ff.) makes a difference between position-related individual replacement costs and person-related replacement costs.

From the current point of view, the Mr. Schulze's "replacement costs" would sum up to € 20,158.75. Taking these replacement costs as a calculative basis, the corresponding write-offs are calculated for the human resource's expected useful life. Past or future wage and salary payments are not considered within this approach, as they don't have investment character.

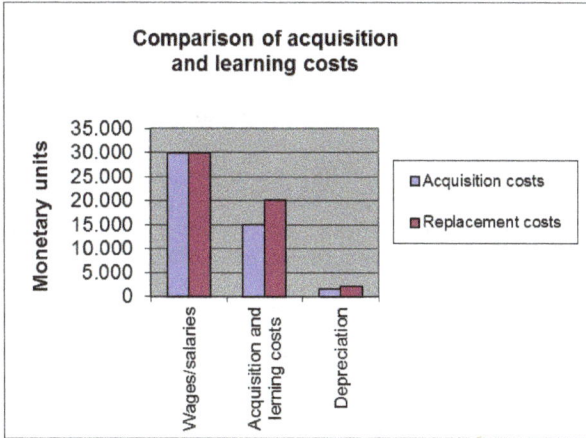

Illustr. 11: Comparison of the acquisition and replacement cost methods

This illustration shows that only investment expenses in human beings are capitalized, but no wages or salaries. Despite the fact that absolute replacement costs generally are higher than the original acquisition costs, the capitalized elements of staff costs do not really result higher as it would be the case within the framework of the method of historical acquisition costs, because increased acquisition and learning costs as well as risen depreciations are distributed over the whole useful life, too. An important difference to the valuation by historical costs is the calculation of an absolute figure of the replacement costs.

Hekimian/Jones (cf. 1967, 107) point out two deficiencies of the replacement cost method:

1. The top level management can dispose of a special asset it wouldn't reimburse at current costs, as its actual value is higher than its book value.

2. There is possibly no similar substitute for a certain asset (e.g. due to the change in technology).

According to Hekimian and Jones (cf. 1967, 107), the method of replacement costs does not only consider costs which are caused by organizational members, but also such ones attributed to the acquisition and training of other organizational members, provided that the costs were essential for the employment of a certain organizational member. The following example illustrates this:

30 engineers are taken on by a company. In the company, they get further training courses. Some of them retire over time. Finally, four competent engineers remain within the company, one of them being an outstanding designer. To replace him by a person with the same qualification and experience, 30 new engineers would have to be taken on again.

In the above mentioned example, it is left aside how probable it is to find a designer of "the same kind and quality"; the replacement costs would be huge, and the question arises to which extent the calculated replacement costs would reflect the real circumstances. Besides, costs for other organizational members would be recorded not only once, but several times during the assessment of individual HR values. The reason for this is that the boundaries of costs for other organizational members wouldn't be possible. To solve this problem, Aschoff and Flamholtz suggest that only individual expenses with investment character should be capitalized, and not such ones caused by the employment and the fluctuation of other organizational members. For reasons of plausibility and practicability, this suggestion is laid down as a basis for the method of replacement costs in this work. However, the method of replacement costs contains the following disadvantages:

- difficulty in determining an absolute replacement figure
- subjectivity of data acquisition (no real replacement takes place; on the contrary, the calculation of theoretical replacement costs are strictly based upon an arithmetical analysis)

As a consequence of the above mentioned disadvantages, this HR-assessment concept is less suitable for open company reporting, but can merely be used for the internal personnel management, e.g. in replacement cases within the area of staff recruitment (cf. Bösch 1979, 20ff).

3.1.3 Opportunity Cost Method

The opportunity cost method[6] is based upon the assumption that assets or resources are scarce goods that only have a value if there is a possible alternative use for them (cf. Hekimian/Jones 1967, 108). The objective of this method is not only the optimal allocation of human resources within the company by means of a "quasi market mechanism", but also to attain a stronger motivation of the managerial staff and to find out and develop the "value" of a firm's employees (cf. Schoenfeld 1974, 12). By the use of this method, the total profit of the company shall get maximized. Both in companies and in the civil service, many people are busy with jobs in which their contribution to overall performance is considerably lower than this would be the case in other jobs or if these employees were involved with more challenging tasks in the organization (cf. Hekimian/Jones 1967, 111). Hekimian and Jones (cf. 1967, 111) assume that these "waste costs", illustrated by lost benefits of the organization, also lead to frustration, or to a decrease in the employees' performance. The following requirements have to be met when using the opportunity cost method in the civil service:

- subdivision of the company into at least two investment centers
- the investment centers' heads' competition for the same employees or the same staff group
- the heads' of department awareness of the fact that their success is assessed by the effected capital return (ROI)
- determination of a target interest rate on capital by the corporate management
- assessment of all tangible assets at market prices

Beyond that, the following premises are laid down for this method (cf. Schoenfeld 1974, 12f): First of all, there should be no valuation for employees who could be easily replaced from outside the company. Second, the valuation of scarce goods is determined by internal bidding (for instance, a scarcity situation only exists if an employee's occupation at his workspace leads to him lacking elsewhere). A department manager will submit the highest bid for an employee if he has the highest profit expectations regarding the employee's future employment.

---

[6] This method is also called the "Competitive Bidding Model" (cf. Ladda et al. 2001, 7).

By means of the opportunity cost method, the value of human assets is calculated as follows (cf. Schoenfeld 1974, 13):

$$V_{Mg} = \frac{Gi \pm Ge}{Rs} \times 100$$

$$V_{Md} = [\frac{Ge}{Rs} \times 100] - V_i$$

V_{Mg} = maximum bid to keep the target profit on the basis of marginal capital

V_{Md} = maximum bid to keep the target profit on the basis of overall capital

G_i = actual profit

G_e = expected profit

R_s = target profit

V_i = market value of tangible assets

The following example illustrates the HR assessment by the opportunity cost method:

	department A	department B
Market value of tangible assets (V_i)	1,000,000	2,000,000
Actual profit (absolute figure) (G_i)	300,000	160,000
Actual profit (relative figure) (R_i)	30 %	8 %
Target profit (relative figure) (R_s)	15 %	10 %
Expected profit after engaging 8 engineers (G_e)	--	300,000
Expected profit after dismissing 8 engineers (G_e)	200,000	--
Maximum bid to keep the target profit on the basis of marginal capital (V_{Mg})	667,000	1,400,000
Maximum bid to keep the target profit on the basis of overall capital (V_{Md})	1,000,000	1,000,000

Illustr. 12: Maximum bids for employees in euros[7]

Reviewing this assessment approach, the following problems arise (cf. Beyer 1991, 162):

- Due to the evaluation of scarce goods on the basis of an internal scarcity concept, this method is extremely subjective (higher subjectivity in comparison to usual market scarcity).

---

[7] Following Schoenfeld 1974, 13, and Hekimian/Jones 1967, 109.

- The method is almost not feasible, as the required "auction" can only lead to evaluations in very rare cases. For example, specialists are not mobile within firms. Therefore, they are not assessed, whereas "less often" needed generalists are recorded, even if they can be replaced in the market).
- Wages/salaries are not taken into account.

Furthermore, the impacts on the employees' work ethics cannot be foreseen within the framework of this method. What is more, it can also be discussed whether this method can replace a market or not, and whether wages and salaries can be left out of account or not. In addition to that, the following questions concerning the opportunity cost method remain unanswered (cf. Hekimian/Jones 1967, 110-111):

1. How are salaries with investment character treated in contrast to such ones without investment character?
2. How are training costs credited between "surrendering" and "accepting" business unit?
3. To what extent shall the expected period of employment be taken into account?
4. How often and how (openly or secretly) shall fictitious auctions take place?
5. Which minimum profit rate is laid down as a basis?
6. How have write-offs to be made from the once determined values?
7. How can the evaluation's negative psychological effect on the employees be avoided or compensated?

While in macroeconomic terms, the opportunity cost method is built up upon flawless proceedings, from the business management's point of view, it appears to be unsuitable in this form (cf. Schoenfeld 1974, 13). Despite these objections, the opportunity cost method can be considered as a worthwhile contribution to the scientific discussion in the field of human resource assessment.

3.1.4 Valuation on Future Costs

There are two different concepts for the assessment of human resources on the basis of future costs: While Hermanson's adjusted discounted future wages model takes into account personnel costs of the following five years, and weights them according to their proximity to a certain point of reference, the method of future earnings is an attempt to calculate the cash value of future earnings on the basis of a probability factor and by a prognosis of the professional life. Henceforth, both assessment methods will be presented in theory and by means of examples.

3.1.4.1 The Adjusted Discounted Future Wages Model

As a company's constant contribution to staff maintenance, wages and salaries of the following five years are the basis of the adjusted discounted future wages model (cf. Hermanson 1964, 15-17). Taking the increase in staff costs and an average interest rate of e.g. 6% as a basis, the reckoned future staff costs are first discounted to their present value:

Wages and salaries p.a. in €	Discount factor (r = 6%)	Present value in €
100,000	0.943	94,300
120,000	0.890	106,800
135,000	0.840	113,400
140,000	0.792	110,880
150,000	0.747	112,050
		537,430

Tab. 1: Discounted annual wages and salaries[8]

To put more emphasis on the income of the recent years, the years closer to the point of reference are stressed more than the years of the far past. Therefore, a so-called "efficiency ratio" is calculated on the basis of the past five years. This ratio is a comparison of the annual in-house efficiency (R_{ij}) with the average efficiency of the branch or line of industry (R_{dj}); for $J = 1, 2, \ldots, n$ years (cf. Schoenfeld 1974, 11). It represents a company's "asset earning power" compared to the line of business or industry, and, according to Aschoff (cf. 1978, 185), is calculated the following way:

---

[8] Following Schoenfeld 1974, 11.

$$ER = [5\,\frac{R_{i1}}{R_{d1}} + 4\,\frac{R_{i2}}{R_{d2}} + 3\,\frac{R_{i3}}{R_{d3}} + 2\,\frac{R_{i4}}{R_{d4}} + 1\,\frac{R_{i5}}{R_{d5}} +] : 15$$

ER = efficiency ratio
R_{ij} = profitability of the company
R_{dj} = average efficiency of the line of business or industry

The capitalized value of human assets results from performance experiences in the past and from the multiplication of the calculated efficiency ratio by the current, depreciated value of wage and salary payments of the following five years (cf. Schoenfeld 1974, 12).

With the previously assessed current cash value of future remuneration, an efficiency ratio of 1,4 or 0,74 results in the following HR evaluations:

efficiency ratio	value of human assets
1.4	€ 537,430 x 1,4 = € 732,403
0.75	€ 537,430 x 0,75 = € 404,073

Tab. 2: Value of human assets in an analysis period of 5 years (Adjusted discounted future wages model)

The gap between the present value of future remuneration and the current value of human assets is called the "Excess Worth Created by Relatively Efficient Human Resources" (briefly "excess value") by Hermanson (cf. Aschoff 1978, 186). If this value is negative, it implies that there are unexploited human resources:

efficiency ratio	excess value
1.4	€ 732,403 - € 537,430 = € 214,972
0.75	€ 404,073 - € 537,430 = € 134,357

Tab. 3:Excess value in an analysis period of 5 years (Adjusted discounted future wages model)

In the above mentioned example, there are only "positive excess values" in both cases. This means that there are no unexploited human resources. Hermanson is of the opinion that the value of human resources, or at least its changes, can be assessed by comparing the present weighted value with the unweighted one (cf. Hermanson 1964, 7). However, Aschoff (cf. 1978, 187) argues that this way, the value of human resources is considerably determined by the number of accounted periods. For instance, if we only consider three instead of five years, the following human values and "excess values" result:

efficiency ratio	value of human assets	excess value
1.4	€ 314,500 x 1,4 = € 440,300	€ 440,300 - € 314,500 = € 125,800
0.75	€ 314,500 x 0,75 = € 235,875	€ 235,875 - € 314,500 = € (-78,625)

Tab. 4: Human value and "excess value" in an analysis period of 3 years (Adjusted discounted future wages model)

In the above mentioned example, the dependence of human resource values on the respective analysis period becomes apparent: While considering an analysis period of five years still results in positive excess values, an analysis period of three years, though, only leads to a negative excess value. By definition, this is an indicator for unexploited human resources. Therefore, the adjusted discounted future wages model involves the following problems (cf. Aschoff 1978, 187):

- The human resource values strongly depend on the chosen analysis period.
- the prognosis of future wages and salaries
- the determination of an efficiency ratio

Furthermore, it is a problem that the notion of "staff costs" is not clearly defined (cf. Schoenfeld 1974, 12).

3.1.4.2 Method of Future Earnings

The basis of this accounting method[9] is the assumption that *future employee earnings* are a good approximation to determine a company's human assets (cf. Schoenfeld 1974, 14). In this context, HR values should be determined by means of income expectations of larger employee groups, provided that for these groups, future income profiles can be developed graphically or mathematically, and according to age (cf. Lev and Schwartz 1971, 105). If human assets are calculated by means of the method of future earnings, the following guideline would be

---

[9] This method is also called the "Economic Model" or the "Lev & Schwartz Model" (cf. Laddo et al. 2011, 16).

recommendable (cf. Schoenfeld 1974, 14): At first, it has to be examined whether employees belong to certain employee groups. In a further step, it must be analyzed whether future income profiles can be put down graphically or mathematically according to the age of the group members. After this, the determination of each employee's remaining time in the company takes place, with the maximum limit of retirement age. As an employee doesn't always remain in the same company until his retirement, the remaining working time (T – t with T = retirement age, and t = age of the employee) must be weighted with a probability factor P_t (P_t = expected working time of an employee of t years) (cf. Schoenfeld 1974, 15). After the individual remaining working time has been calculated, the probable individual income expectations can be determined with the aid of statistics (cf. Schoenfeld 1974, 14):

$$L* (T\text{-}t) = f\,[L°(T\text{-}t)]$$

L* = income expectations of an individual (according to statistical values for the whole group L°)

The next step is to discount the amount of future earnings to the reference point by means of an interest factor r. The latter has been worked out over a certain period of time. After this, the individual human resource value V of a t year old employee can be calculated from the discounted future wage and salary payments, and from the weighted remaining working time in the company:

$$E\,(V_t)\; = \sum_{t}^{T} P_t \sum_{t}^{T} (\frac{LtT\,(t)}{1-r})^{T-t}$$

The overall value of a company's human assets results from the total of the calculated individual assets or group values. As it is shown below, the assessment of human resources by means of the method of future earnings works as follows:

Mr. Schmidt, employed as a toolmaker in company X (500 employees), is 35 years old. The firm has been existing for 50 years, and it employs 30 toolmakers all in all. What is Mr. Schmidt's human resource value?

1. Mr. Schmidt belongs to the employee group of toolmakers.
2. As the firm has been existing for five decades, income profiles can be derived age-relatedly, graphically, and mathematically for this group. According to a works agreement, an annual wage adjustment of 2% as well as an age-dependent loyalty

donation of 1.5% of the adjusted wage level, are paid. Holiday money isn't paid. The point of departure for the calculation is the initial salary of € 1,200,- of a journeyman aged 18. The current annual wages are calculated as follows:

$$[(€\ 1{,}200x\ (1.02)^{\,n})] \times 1.015^{\,m}] \times 13$$

3. Mr. Schmidt's remaining working time is **30 years** at most (= 65 years (age of retirement) less 35 years (present age)).

4. The probability factor for the remaining working time (0.77 in the present case) is taken from internal statistics. The weighted expectation of Mr. Schmidt's working time is **23.1 years** (= 30 years x 0.77)

5. The calculation of future earnings results from the following income profile:

age	Years of employment after the 18th birthday	Wage developments depending on the age Annual wages (13 wages p.a.)	Discount factor with i = 6.5%	Cash values with i = 6.5%	Accumulated cash values
...					
35 (Mr. Schmidt)	17	28,135.25			
36	18	29,128.32	0.9390	27,351.49	27,351.49
37	19	30,156.62	0.8817	26,589.09	53,940.58
38	20	31,221.06	0.8278	25,844.79	79,785.37
39	21	32,323.26	0.7773	25,124.87	104,910.24
40	22	33,464.27	0.7299	24,425.57	129,335.81
41	23	34,645.55	0.6853	23,742.60	153,078.41
42	24	35,868.54	0.6435	23,081.41	176,159.82
43	25	37,134.70	0.6042	22,436.79	198,596.61
44	26	38,445.56	0.5674	21,814.01	220,410.62
45	27	39,802.69	0.5327	21,202.89	241,613.51
46	28	41,207.72	0.5002	20,612.10	258,427.70
47	29	42,662.35	0.4697	20,038.51	279,039.80
48	30	44,168.33	0.4410	19,478.23	299,078.31
49	31	45,727.48	0.4141	18,935.75	318,556.54
50	32	47,341.66	0.3888	18,406.44	337,492.29
51	33	49,012.86	0.3651	17,894.60	355,898.73
52	34	50,742.97	0.3428	17,394.69	373,793.33
53	35	52,234.20	0.3219	16,814.19	391,188.02
54	36	54,388.62	0.3022	16,436.24	407,624.26
55	37	56,308.57	0.2838	15,980.37	423,604.63
56	38	58,296.27	0.2665	15,535.96	439,140.59
57	39	60,354.12	0.2502	15,100.60	454,241.19
58	40	62,484.62	0.2349	14,677.64	468,918.83
59	41	64,690.33	0.2206	14,270.69	483,189.52

60	42	66,973.90	0.2071	13,870.29	497,059.81
61	43	69,338.08	0.1945	13,486.26	510,546.07
62	44	71,785.71	0.1826	13,108.07	523,654.14
63	45	74,319.75	0.1715	12,745.84	536,399.98
64	46	76,943.24	0.1610	12,387.86	548,787.84
65	47	79,659.32	0.1512	12,044.49	560,832.33

Tab. 5: Table for the individual calculation of cash values (method of future earnings)

6. 23.1 (Mr. Schmidt's weighted working life expectation) x € 560,832.33 (amount of discounted future wages) = **€ 12,955,226.82= Mr. Schmidt's human resource value**

Although the assessment of human resources by means of the method of future earnings appears to be relatively easy at first sight, the following problems arise when reviewing this method (cf. Flamholtz 1973, 73 ff, and Schoenfeld 1974, 15f):

- In general, an employee's assignment to a certain group seems to be difficult.
- Statistics on particular staff groups don't necessarily reflect the real business facts.
- Future earnings don't always reflect the real employee's value for a business, as the earnings consist of various components for which different factors like skills and ability (bargaining skills) are determining (cf. Hekimian/Jones 1967, 106).
- The discount and probability factors are controversial.
- The possibility of leaving a business for other reasons but retirement is left out of consideration.
- Expenses for apprenticeship, further training, and all other efforts of the staff management remain unconsidered.
- The possibility of job changes within a business is ignored.
- Group-dynamic processes are not taken into account when adding up single HR values to a company's overall HR values.
- Employment "above value" or "under value" is not recorded, as only the group assignment is relevant for the assessment of human resources.

Furthermore, the application of the method of future earnings isn't possible without the use of a suitable software system, as manual calculations involve the risk of miscalculation because of the probability and discount factors.

3.2 Output-oriented Human Resource Accounting Methods

While input-oriented methods to assess a company's human resources focus on the real or theoretical costs of the past, present or future, output-oriented methods take into account above-average profits of the current period as well as future benefit contributions of organizational members and their behavior as the basis for the assessment of human resources. In the following section, the goodwill method, the method of future contributions to performance as well as the behavioral model will be presented as output-oriented methods of human resources' assessment.

3.2.1 The Goodwill Method

Apart from the adjusted discounted future wages model, the goodwill method was the earliest attempt to determine and to monetarily assess operational human resources (cf. Aschoff 1978, 180). Both methods are attributed to Hermanson. They are based upon the idea that all company resources contribute to firm profit – irrespective whether they are recorded on balance sheets or not (cf. Aschoff 1978, 160 and 180).

The goodwill method is based upon the assumption that the part of the corporate business results exceeding the sector average derives from an asset that is not recorded on the balance sheet. This asset considered as some kind of "original goodwill" (unpurchased goodwill), originating from outstandingly qualified employees; therefore, it is the amount stated for human resources (cf. Schoenfeld 1974, 9).

For the assessment of human resources by means of the goodwill method, the following guideline is recommendable: First, the company's returns of the current period must be determined; in contrast to the adjusted discounted future wages model, only the profits of the current period provide a basis for the assessment of human beings (cf. Aschoff 1978, 180, and Hermanson 1964, 7ff.). However, the goodwill method does not take into account future returns because of their uncertainty, and past profits remain out of consideration in order not to record assets that possibly are already eaten up, and therefore are of no importance for the future of the company (cf. Aschoff 1978, 181). After converting stated tangibles into market prices, the calculation of a company-specific profitability rate of the current year takes place: For this purpose, the actual profit is compared with the market value of the tangibles (cf. Schoenfeld 1974, 9). Then, the business-specific, above-average part of the profit (i.e. the "surplus or excess profit") or the below-average profit (i.e. the "reduced profit") is calculated by comparing the business-specific profitability rate with the sector's profitability rate. In the next step, the resulting amount of excess or reduced profit is capitalized at the sector's profitability. Finally, this reveals the value of human capital or human assets (cf. Schoenfeld 1974, 9).

The assessment of human assets by means of the goodwill method is illustrated in the following example (cf. Schoenfeld 1974, 10):

	factory B1	factory B2	factory B3	average
market value of tangible assets (V_i)	100,000	50,000	150,000	100,000
actual profit (G_i)	15,000	5,000	4,000	8,000
actual profit in % of the tangible assets (R_i)	15%	10%	2.6%	8% R_d
Difference from the average profit [G_{di} = (R_i - R_d) x V_i]	7,000	1,000	-8,000	--
Human assets (V_m) = "excess assets" or "reduced assets" (G_{di} : R_d) x 100	**87,500**	**12,500**	**-100,000**	--

Tab. 6: Illustration of human assets by means of the goodwill method

Comparing the factories B1, B2 and B3, we realize that the excess value in factory B1 (87.500 monetary units) represents the biggest amount, and that it originates from human assets. In contrast to this, we have a reduced value of –100,000 monetary units in factory B3. B2 takes a position in between, accounting for 12,500 monetary units.

However, the goodwill method has the following deficiencies (cf. Schoenfeld 1974, 10):

- gathering annual changes compared with the sector's average instead of assessing the basic amount of human assets
- The calculated exceeding amount of the business profit is only attributed to human resources. Hermanson claims – although without evidence – that the

biggest part of these "excess assets" is attributed to human resources (cf. Hermanson 1964, 14).

- Problems with the calculation of reliable branch profitability rates and with the calculation of the exceeding value part in different branches.
- No clarification of the origins nor of the attribution of negative human asset values (as for example their allocation to tangible assets, or their treatment as loss carried forward)

3.2.2 Assessment Based on Future Performance

Between 1964 and 1974, the view caught on that the whole future economic use – and not the original acquisition values – represented the real value of an asset:

> Assets represent expected future economic benefits, rights to which have been acquired by the enterprise as a result of some current or past transactions (Sprouse/Moonitz, 1962, 2).

According to Schoenfeld (1974, 15f), assets only exist

> wenn zum Beispiel eine Dienstleistung oder ein anderer Nutzen dem Betrieb ganz oder teilweise mit hohem Wahrscheinlichkeitsgrad zufließen wird.

From these ideas, the following valuation approaches of human assets evolved.

3.2.2.1   Method of Future Contributions to Performance

The method of future contributions to performance takes the organizational member's future contributions for the gross performance of the business into account; these contributions are considered as crucial for the assessment of human resources (cf. Schoenfeld 1974, 16).

The value of human resources is determined both by characteristics of the organization and the employee himself. In this respect, this assessment concept differs from all up to now mentioned Human Resource Accounting concepts. Neither the projection of staff payments by means of the method of future earnings, nor the capture or simulation of market values by means of the opportunity cost method make it possible to find out individual future contributions to performance. Schoenfeld (cf. 1974, 16) is of the opinion that a reliable HR assessment is probably only possible for single cases with their respective peculiarities; only then, all special or business-specific developments and changes can be taken into account. This is the case with the method of future contributions to performance.

There are two ways of assessment for this method: While by means of the first model, the possible future change of an employee' hierarchy levels remains unconsidered, the member of an organization is "allowed" to take different hierarchy levels in the firm within the framework of the so-called "Stochastic Rewards Valuation Model".

3.2.2.1.1 Method of Future Contributions without Hierarchy Levels

The basis of this method is the assumption that the performance of each employee is realized by assessable future contributions to overall performance. This depends on the following three factors (cf. Schoenfeld 1974, 16):

- the position of the organizational member in the business (k)
- the performance level of the organizational member in a certain job (l)
- the employee's remaining time in each position (t)

After weighting these factors with probabilities, the expected future performance contribution is calculated in terms of an expected value E (V) as an approximate value for human resources (cf. Schoenfeld 1974, 17). The arithmetical calculation works as follows:

$$(E_V) = \sum_{k=1}^{K} \sum_{l=1}^{L} \sum_{t=1}^{T} (S_{klt} P\{S_{klt}\})$$

As the value of human resources is not only influenced by characteristics of the organizational member, but also by the organization itself, all influences on the performance of organizational members have to be considered to assess human assets. Influences of the organization might, for instance, consist of the organizational structure or of the management style of superiors (cf. Schoenfeld 1974, 17). On the whole, there is a great variety of organizational influences on individuals which can hardly be quantified in a business.

When reviewing the above mentioned assessment method, the following problems become apparent (cf. Schoenfeld 1974, 17):

- Sometimes, the evaluation of probabilities is only possible for a bigger amount of employees.
- Sometimes, the forecast of future contributions to performance is unreliable.
- The estimation and assessment of an organizational member's contributions to a company's overall performance requires the valuation of future earnings of the whole business as well as the "cost share" among all involved production factors.
- Considering all influences on an organizational member's performance is not feasible.

Even if this method represents a well-discussed assessment approach in literature, Flamholtz doesn't consider it to be suitable for practical use (cf. Flamholtz 1971, 253 – 263). As a reason for this, he points out that for instance individual probabilities, even if they are determined exactly, are not useful because of their broad distribution (cf. Flamholtz 1973, 82 ff.). Nevertheless, with the aid of this method, Flamholtz tries to show a way for the further development of illustrating human assets in company reporting; furthermore, he wants to outline problems occurring in this context (cf. Schoenfeld 1974, 16).

3.2.2.1.2   The Stochastic Rewards Valuation Model

A further variation of this method is the so-called "Stochastic Rewards Valuation Model", also based upon the evaluation of expected future performance contributions of an organizational member. It includes the idea that an employee can take different positions and hierarchy levels during his working life in a company. Furthermore, it takes into account that individual performance can vary in quality and quantity. Within this assessment model, human assets depend on the following factors:

- the employee's expected years of service

- succession of positions and hierarchy levels that an employee can take within his years of service
- performance level in the respective positions

The mathematical expectation of the individual human asset results from adding up and discounting all expected future contributions to performance for the employee's remaining years of service. The amount of all individual human assets results in the overall amount of HR values of a business.

The determination of human resource values by means of the Stochastic Rewards Valuation Model takes place in five steps (cf. Gebauer/Wall 2002, 688):

1. Identification of all potentially attainable hierarchy levels
2. Analysis of an organizational member's potential future contributions to overall performance at each hierarchy level
3. Individual estimation of the remaining years of service at future hierarchy levels for each organizational member
4. Weighting the different number of remaining years of service with probabilities
5. Adding up individual human resource values to the overall amount of human assets at a business' disposal

Apart from the already mentioned niggles in the context of the "Method of future contributions to performance", the Stochastic Rewards Valuation Model also contains the problem of assessing an employee's potential future positions at different hierarchy levels.

However, this accounting method represents a consequent orientation towards future values; nevertheless, the prognosis of a lot of data is necessary to account human assets this way (cf. Gebauer/Wall 2002, 688). Gebauer and Wall (cf. 2002, 688) consider the monetary assessment of employees performance to be possible; the forecast of entire career paths, though, contains considerable problems. A solution of this method's problems is still to be awaited; on top of everything, a general draft should hardly be found. Even if the Stochastic Rewards Valuation

Model has already been applied as a prototype, its broader distribution rather seems improbable at its actual stage of development (cf. Gebauer/Wall 2002, 688).

3.2.2.2   The Behavioral Model

The basis of the behavioral model or the method of behavior variables is the assumption that a company's functioning social relationship system highly contributes to its overall performance (cf. Schoenfeld 1974, 24). Therefore, this system is of great value for the organization. However, the special meaning of such a system only becomes apparent if the same overall performance of an organization could be also reached without this relationship system.

While in accountancy, investments and their results often are measured by expenses spent on them in terms of profitability, cost effectiveness, and other dimensions, and while it is believed that a cause-and-effect relationship exists between an investment and its results, there are still other figures with a considerable influence on the results – apart from the variables usually used for investment calculation: The so-called "causal variable", and "intervening variable". Factors like an organizational member's level of skills and competences, the behavior both of the management and of equals as well as the organizational structure belong to the "causal variable"; factors of the "intervening variable" are, for instance, attitude, motivation, communication, skills, and possibilities of interaction, abilities of problem solving and acting, the health of organizational members and relationships between employees. Despite their essential influence on the result situation, causal and intervening variables usually are not taken into account within the company's information system, nor are they considered within investment calculations.

In order to observe and control those variables that considerably influence on the operating income, the factors belonging to causal and intervening variables need a constant supervision. With regard to the usually recorded data in a business, this means that the relevant scope of data has to be considerably enhanced within the context of the behavioral model. Schoenfeld (cf. 1974, 24-25) compiles all variables with an influence on human assets as follows:

management's information needs on resources

information on acquisition development	information on status and maintenance	information and on use (employment)
- issue cost	"book value"	- economic value
- replacement costs		

investment variable →	causal variable →	intervening variable →	result variable →	return on investment variable
human resources: 1. cost of each individual: • engagement • training • introduction • general further development 2. Cost for system start, system development	Level of skills and competences of each individual	Synergetic conditions: - attitude - motivation - communication - interaction facilities (skills) - problem solving skills, means of action - health - employee relationships	productivity costs quality return net cash flow	Return-on-Investment per employee
	Type of ... ... management behavior ... the behavior of equals towards one another ... the organizational structure			Return-on-Investment (interacting system)

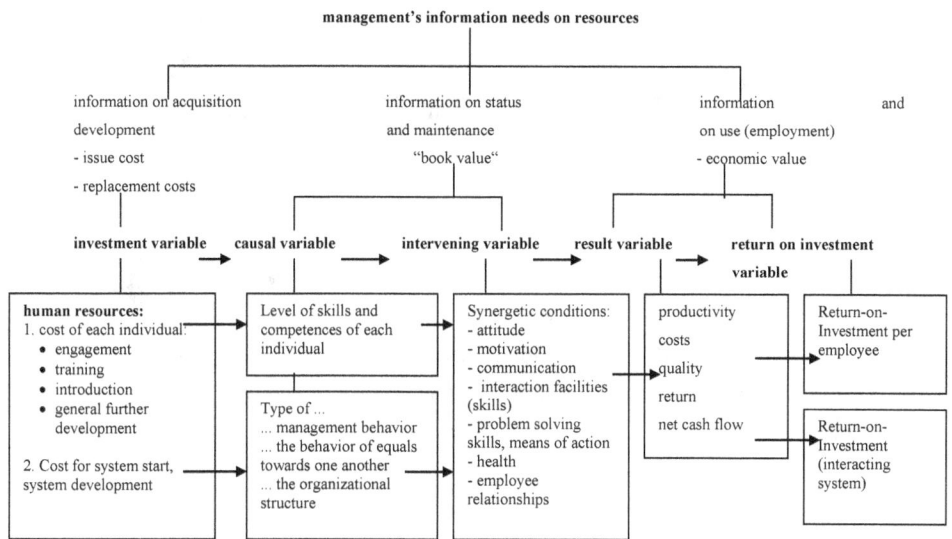

Illustr. 13: Factors involved with human assets (behavioral model)

According to Likert, human assets V can be represented as a function of the causal variable X_i at the moment t, of the intervening variable Y_i at the moment t, and the resulting variable Z_i at the moment t within the context of this approach (cf. Schoenfeld 1974, 24-26):

$$V_t = f[X_{it}; Y_{it}; Z_{it}]$$

The special meaning of this method will be demonstrated in the following example (cf. Likert/Bowers 1973, 15-24):

Because of an improved order situation, company A and B have increased their training efforts. However, because of the change in management behavior, the working atmosphere has worsened in company B. In company A, the causal and intervening variables remained stable. The corresponding impacts on human resources are the following ones:

Assessment approach for human resources	Impacts on human resources	
	Company A	Company B
Behavioral model	Preservation or increase of human assets	Decrease of human assets
Cost value method	Increase of human assets	Increase of human assets

Tab. 7: Comparison of the impacts of the behavioral model and the Cost value method on human assets)

Within the context of the behavioral model, a worsened working atmosphere generally leads to a decrease in human assets because of a negative change of causal and intervening variables (cf. Illustr. 14); yet, within the context of the cost value method, an increase of human assets can be stated (cf. Schoenfeld 1974, 26).

Change of structure or process

(causal variable)

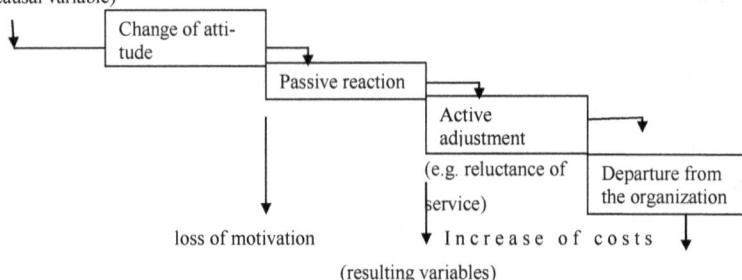

Illustr. 14: Stages of a decrease in social potenial[10]

In the middle of the seventies of the past century, the need to gather all influencing factors on human resources came up, as it was believed that it would never be completely possible to show those changes of this production factor which were not directly linked to expenditures[11] (cf. Schoenfeld 1974, 26). Up to now, the big amount of factors contributing to social relation systems in organizations could not be measured. However, without the full awareness of those factors and their links, neither the assessment of the value, nor of value changes of organizational social

---

[10] Cf.. Marr 1982, 564.

[11] "[...] Veränderungen dieses Produktionsfaktors, die nicht mit direkten Aufwendungen verbunden sind" (Schoenfeld 1974, 26).

relationship systems is possible[12]. What is more, correct statements about causal variables between investments in staff, staff behavior, and operational performance results can only refer to a narrow range of space and time at the present level of behavioral science (cf. Fischer 1999, 37/38). On the one hand, this is attributed to the indirect measurability of links between behavior-stimulating influences on staff, on the other hand, this is ascribed to behavioral results (cf. Szyperski 1962, 67-83, and Fischer 1999, 38).

When reviewing the behavioral model, the following problems of this method arise (cf. Schoenfeld 1974, 24-26):

- gathering and defining the scope of causal and intervening variables
- gathering and quantitatively evaluating links and link strengths between single variables with regard to overall results
- neglect of different characters and different reactions of organizational members towards changes in causal and intervening variables
- collecting and reflecting temporally-delayed effects as a consequence of changes in causal and intervening variables

In literature, the behavioral model is not picked up and treated further. Nor could an example for practical application be found for this theoretical approach. For this reason, we must assume that efforts in this field towards the further development of this approach were not successful.

---

[12] As an attempt to assess human resources remains incomplete without considering these components, Likert stresses the need to establish correlations between causal variable, intervening variable and resulting variable within organizations (cf. Likert/Bowers 1973, 15-24, and Schoenfeld 1974, 24).

4. Status Quo and requirements regarding a Human Resource Accounting System in the German land Hesse

In this chapter, it will be analyzed at first whether methods of Human Resource Accounting (HRA) are already being applied in the civil service of Hesse. In a second step, Hesse's current requirements for a Human Resource Accounting system in its public administration will be examined, before the general requirements for a functioning Human Resource Accounting System will be highlighted. After this, the stakeholders' demands towards an HRA-system in Hesse's civil service are the focal point of interest. In the end, the gap between the current situation in Hesse and the requirements for Human Resource Accounting in the Hessian Civil Service will round this chapter off.

4.1 Status Quo of Human Resource Accounting in Hesse's Civil Service

The present budget position of the land Hesse is, like the one of the Federal Republic of Germany (briefly "Bund"), of other German states, and numerous municipalities, generally marked by a high absolute debt repayment status. Furthermore, a debt brake has been introduced to rule out new borrowings as of 2020[13].

Considering the last two decades, the Hesse's absolute debt level at first increased from about DM 33,22 Mio. (about € 16,99 Mio.) in 1993 to about € 25,68 Mio.[14] at the end of 2002 (cf. Hessisches Ministerium der Finanzen 2003, and Seilheimer

---

[13] According to ss. 109 III cl. 5, 143d I cl. 3 GG, the German states must do without new borrowings as of 2020 (cf. Frese 2012, 153). There is a difference between states with and without Consolidation Aids: According to s. 1 of the Consolidation Aid Act, the German states Berlin, Bremen, Saarland, Saxony-Anhalt and Schleswig-Holstein can get annual Consolidation Aids of 800 million of euros altogether on the basis of an administrative agreement for the period form 2011 up to 2012. The amount is financed by the Federal Budget (cf. Sekretariat des Stabilitätsrates 2012, 1. While states with Consolidation Aids are obliged to cut back their financing deficit until 2019 (cf. Frese 2012, 154), the cutback of structural new indebtedness of the other states until 2020 depends on the political will; sanctions are not provided (cf. Frese 2012, 154).

[14] This corresponds with relative new borrowings of 51.15% in the indicated period of time.

2007, 61). Seilheimer (cf. 2007, 61) gives an overview of the absolute debt positions from 1993 to 2002, and she indicates the corresponding relative new borrowings in a year-on-year view, too[15]. The corresponding situation for the period of 2000 to 2009[16] respectively 2012[17] is shown below:

year	absolute debt level in Mio. €	Debts per inhabitant in €	relative new borrowings (in %), year-on-year
2000	22,483	3,712	
2001	23,791	3,918	5.817729
2002	25,679	4,221	7.935774
2003	28,037	4,605	9.1826006
2004	29,441	4,836	5.0076684
2005	31,000	5,088	5.2953364
2006	30,084	4,950	-2.954839
2007	30,626	5,045	1.8016221
2008	31,178	5,137	1.8023901
2009	33,997	5,610	9.0416319
2010[18]	37.694	6.216	10,8744889
2011[19]	39.471	6.497	4,7142781

Tab. 8: Debt levels of Hesse (2000-2011)

---

[15] Yet, according to the Hessisches Ministerium der Finanzen (2003), inflationary developments are not indicated.

[16] Cf. Hessisches Statistisches Landesamt 2012, 1.

[17] According to the Hessisches Statistisches Landesamt (cf. 2012, 1), the status of inhabitants on June 30 is relevant in each case.

[18] In 2010, an important adjustment of the debt statistics was conducted by the German Federal Statistical Office. As a consequence of this, the figures of up to the year 2009 are only partly comparable with the figures of the year 2010 and later ones, cf. Burth 2011, 1. So the figure of € 44,734 Mio. includes debt guarantees and other public funds, institutions, and enterprises (cf. Burth 2011, 1), the one of 43,705 excludes debt guarantees, but includes public funds, institutions, and enterprises (cf. Burth 2011, 1). However, the figures indicated subsequently are comparable with the ones of the previous year, as it neither includes debt guarantees nor other public funds, institutions, and enterprises (cf. Hessisches Statistisches Landesamt 2012a).

[19] Hessisches Statistisches Landesamt 2012a. The data of 2012 are collected on 31st December 2012, and there is no current data avaliable in the Statistical Office of Hesse, cf. Hessisches Statistisches Landesamt 2012a.

In the following grouping survey of Hesse's budget of the year 2012[20] (grouping of earnings and expenses), it can be realized what kind of expenses are mainly responsible for the extent of overall public expenses:

Main group/super-ordinate group	Kind of expenses	Expenses in €	Share in overall expenses
4 – 9	overall expenses[21]	29,732,702,300	100%
4	staff expenses	8,078,827,200	27.17%[22] (31.52% in 2003)
41	expenses for deputies and honorary capacities	26,833,400	0.09% (0.11%[23] in 2003)
42	remuneration and additional payments	5,418,644,600	18.22% (21.70% in 2003)
43	pensions and suchlike	2,077,200,000	7% (7.49% in 2003)
44	grants, allowances and suchlike	534,247,000	1.8% (1.7% in 2003)
45	other staff-related expenses	21,902,200	0.7% (1.47% in 2003)
46	global extra or lower expenses for personnel	-	- (3.69% in 2003)
5	material administrative expenses, expenses for debt service	7,679,602,000	25.83% (20.89% in 2003)
51 – 54	material administrative expenses	1,349,601,500	4.5% (4.34% in 2003)
56 – 59	expenses for debt service	6,330,000,500 [24]	21.29% (16.55% in 2003)
56	interest spending to territorial authorities, separate estates, and territorial communities (1)	13,362,000	0.04% (1.09% in 2003)
57	interest spending at the credit market (2)	1,487,774,100	5% (6.28% in 2003)
58	Capital repayment to (1)	28,638,000	0.1% (1.76% in 2003)
59	Capital repayment to (2)	4,800,226,400	16.14% (9.99% in 2003)

Tab. 9: Excerpt from Hesse's grouping survey of the budget 2012

[20] Cf. Hessisches Ministerium der Finanzen 2012, 28-32.

[21] [4] "Personalausgaben" € 8,078,827,200,-; [5] "Sächliche Verwaltungsausgaben, Ausgaben für den Schuldendienst" € 7,679,602,000,-; [6] "Ausgaben für Zuweisungen + Zuschüsse mit Ausnahme für Investitionen (€ 9,135,627,200,-); [7] "Baumaßnahmen" (€ 594,121,500,-; [8] "Sonstige Ausgaben für Investitionen + Investitionsfördermaßnahmen" (€ 1,488,937,000,-); [9] "Besondere Finanzierungsausgaben" (€ 2,755,587,400,-), cf. Hessisches Ministerium der Finanzen 2012, 28-32.

[22] The absolute amount of staff expenses was € 6,854,628,600,- in 2003, so the despite the relative decrease in staff expenses in 2012, staff expenses increased up to the indicated figure. (cf. Haushaltsplan Land Hessen 2003, 42ff; Hessisches Ministerium der Finanzen 2012, 28-32; Seilheimer 2007, 62; cf. also note 15). One reason for the relative decrease in staff expenses were reoccupation blocks.

[23] The indicated percentage of 1.1% by Seilheimer 2007, 62 must be adjusted this way.

[24] In 2003, the amount was € 3,599,736,400,-, the share was 16.55%.

The main reason for Hesse's high debt level and the continuous increase of Hesse's river of red ink are the steadily growing redemption and interest payments for credits on the one hand, and the large proportion of staff cost on the overall expenditures on the other hand.

Despite the outstanding role of human resources for task fulfillment in the civil service and in view of the high proportion of staff expenses, the "value" of public employees remains in the dark, and they are not considered as an "asset" by their employers either, but merely recorded as an element of expenditure in the budget of state accounting – despite their outstanding above-mentioned role. The consequence of this is that for the further decrease of Hesse's high debt level, mainly the means of continuous cuts in the areas of human and material resources is used at present. As a consequence of this, even less financial resources are made available for task fulfillment. Up to now, Hesse's government has neither tried to gather the value of its staff by using HRA-methods yet, nor to use the value of human assets as a basis for efficient decision-making or for economic task fulfillment.

4.2 Current Requirements of Hesse's State Administration concerning Human Resource Accounting

As a contribution to the future decrease in total expenditures as well as to the decline of Hesse's public debts, general cutbacks in human and material resources don't only have positive effects, but also lead to frustration, demotivation, and a decrease in employee performance. In order to avoid such negative effects of global financial cutbacks, it would make sense to pave the way for a more efficient use of human resources in the civil service of Hesse. This could be done with the aid of suitable methods of Human Resource Accounting. Therefore, Hesse's requirements for Human Resource Accounting will be presented in the following.

4.2.1 Improved Employee Appreciation

In the Hessian state administration, the factor "personnel" is only recorded as an element of expenditure up to now. This implies that human resources are only regarded as a cost factor, and not as a worthwhile "factor of production". With the creation of a philosophy to consider public servants as valuable resources, a higher employee motivation and commitment could be expected; this would lead to more efficient and thus cost-saving work, and could also contribute to the decrease of the high public debt level. The monetary staff valuation would enhance the appreciation of public service employees in the state administration of Hesse.

4.2.2 Improved Illustration of Hesse's Assets in accounting

The consequence of non-recording human resources as "assets" in cameralistics or rather accounting is that not all resources contributing to the overall performance of an organization are recorded and shown in accounting. In 2007, Seilheimer (cf. 2007, 64) mentioned that, if accounting of the land Hesse, carried out pursuant to s. 71 a LHO, was additionally conducted according to the rules of the Commercial Code ("Handelsgesetzbuch"), the documentation of human assets or tied public funds in the balance sheet (or in an auxiliary calculation) could contribute to improve the illustration of assets in the civil service of Hesse; thus, they could serve as a basis for decision-making in politics and administration. In 2009, state accounting was first conducted according to the rules of the Commercial Code – in an auxiliary calculation, with the aim to record Hesse's material assets. Nevertheless, the "value" of human assets cannot be found anywhere, and human resources only "appear" as an expense item in the traditional cameralistic budget. However, the documentation of human assets in an auxiliary calculation could especially contribute to an increase of quality, transparency, and efficiency in decisions – notably concerning political decisions in the budget and staff areas; in the end, this could lead to a decrease in the huge amount of public spending, and contribute to the goals of the debt break for new borrowings.

4.2.3 Cost Transparency in the Value Chain of the HR Department

The lack of cost transparency, notably within the value chain of the HR department, also represents a significant problem in the Hessian state administration. So in many cases, for instance, it remains unclear which costs arise during selection or recruitment procedures (acquisition costs, learning costs). The consequence of missing cost transparency in the staff recruitment phase is that the costs of this phase are generally not considered enough - with the effect that recruitment costs are usually higher than this would be the case under given cost transparency. For other sections of the value chain in the HR department, there are many examples of missing cost transparency and its involving consequences on inefficient acting. If suitable HRA-methods were transferred to the public sector, accruing staff costs could be recorded and represented systematically. Calculated values could then be used as a basis for decision-making for administrative and political purposes.

A thus created cost transparency in the whole value chain of the cost-intensive personnel sector could also contribute to an improved allocation of public funds and, as a consequence, by a more efficient way of acting of decision-makers, lead to a considerable decrease in total expenditure.

4.2.4 Qualification-oriented Staff Employment

Another problem of Hesse's state administration is, like the one in many other areas of the public service, too, that staff employment doesn't really take up the employees' current qualifications (knowledge, capabilities and skills), but is fundamentally based upon the highest acquired vocational qualification at the moment of the engagement. Further qualifications usually are not considered for the assignment to a certain career group or salary bracket[25]. The consequence of this is that many servants don't get paid for their current qualifications, but are rather employed above their qualifications or, in contrast to this, below them. An employment above standard is given when servants have higher qualifications than needed in their job, whereas a substandard employment is given when the qualifications don't meet the requirements of the actual field of action. The consequences of an above or substandard employment mainly are frustration, demotivation and restraint performance of the persons affected. To mitigate the effects of above or substandard employment, it has to be checked first to what extent staff employment answers qualifications. An improved, qualification-oriented staff employment (within the bounds of public services law), and an involved better recognition of servants can be brought about by means of Human

---

[25] This is particularly the case with servants of the higher intermediate service whose assignment to their original career brackets is common, even if they possess one or more further degrees above their original one. This shows the structural rigidity of the existing HR structures.

Resource Accounting. Apart from the increase in employee motivation, an improved individual performance, a decrease in waste costs as well as a long-term decrease in public expenditure are to be expected as the results of a qualification-oriented staff employment.

4.2.5 The Creation of an Objective Assessment Basis for Promotions and for Incentive Bonuses

A widespread means to cut down expenditures on staff have been reoccupation blocks. Another means to reduce staff expenditures in Hesse's Civil Service was a reduced number of promotions; furthermore, in 1993, 1994, 1996, 1997 and 1998, promotions were postponed to a later date by the Hessian Ministry of the Interior and Sports (cf. Hessischer Landtag 2001, 3-4). The inevitable consequence of this was a more restricted selection of servants considered for following promotion rounds. For promotions, only those servants were and are taken into account who show a positive appraisal by their direct superior[26]. However, the evaluated categories are not measured in an ordinal way, but merely expressed in a language-focused way. Therefore, promotions in the Hessian state administration are regularly conducted on the basis of purely language-based, subjectively issued appraisals. This subjectivity is also given if there are two appraisals of two different superiors after a job rotation. For this reason, servants who did not get promoted cannot always understand on which assessment bases promotions had been pronounced. Among servants who were or are not considered for promotions, this can lead to negative effects both on motivation and willingness to perform. The consequence of this is that the "overall performance" of authorities decreases. In order to conduct promotions on a quantitatively objective assessment basis and to minimize the above mentioned negative effects on motivation and performance, HR assessments should be supported by suitable Human Resource Accounting methods. Then, not promoted servants would have the opportunity to get informed neutrally both on their current human resource values and their deficits; this way, they could also get clues for their further personnel development.

---

[26] The document destined for the staff report contains two main sections: I. Personal and service-related data, II: scope of performance and personality image (assessment of performance features and ability features). The "measurement" relies on literal descriptions and is not arithmetical.

These remarks on promotions can also be transferred to the grant of incentive bonuses in several Hessian state authorities. Incentive bonuses are granted in case the direct superior considers certain employees worthwhile for them, and proposes them for the list of candidates. However, it often remains unclear on which basis such grants take place – in lack of a neutral, objective and comparable assessment basis. This problem could be sorted out by a quantitative HR assessment by means of suitable HRA-methods.

4.3 General Requirements for Human Resource Accounting

In order to apply HRA-methods appropriately in practice, these methods have to meet certain requirements with regard to the quality criteria "objectivity", "reliability" and "validity"; what is more, they must be suitable for use in practice. Only if quality criteria are considered enough, reliable deductions can be drawn out of an analysis (cf. Gabler Wirtschaftslexikon, 1993, 1439). Furthermore, costs accruing because of the use of HRA-methods must be "inevitable" and proportionate to the thus expected advantages.

4.3.1 Objectivity

Measurement methods meet the requirements regarding objectivity if the measurement results are independent of the respective head of examination (cf. Gabler Wirtschaftslexikon 1993, 2447). According to this, HRA-methods are objective if different and independent heads of examination reach the same human resource value. There are three kinds of objectivity:

1. the *objectivity of application* (Ger. *"Durchführungsobjektivität"*) (influence on the examination results through the appearance, the target system and value system of the executor),
2. the *objectivity of evaluation* (Ger. *"Auswertungsobjektivität"*) (particularly given in standardized question items) and
3. the *objectivity of interpretation* (Ger. *"Interpretationsobjektivität"*) (little scope for subjective interpretation by the head of examination).

4.3.2 Reliability

The quality criterion of reliability indicates the attained concordance in repeated measurements, using the same measurement methods in *ceteris paribus*-situations (cf. Gabler Wirtschaftslexikon 1993, 2815). It is often described as the correlation between two test series. HRA-methods meet these reliability requirements if they regularly lead to the same results in more than one application of the same data basis.

4.3.3 Validity

The quality criterion of validity measures whether or to which extent methods actually gauge the construct that should be measured (cf. Gabler Wirtschaftslexikon 1993, 3463). Therefore, HRA-methods are valid if a given aim can be reached with their support. In German language usage, the term "Gültigkeit" (validness, validity) also exists as a synonym for validity. Validity is important for the measurement of not directly observable constructs like motivation and attitude.

4.3.4 Practicability

An indispensable prerequisite for the application of HRA-methods is their adaptability to practical purposes. Without the possibility to practically apply theoretically sound HRA-methods, efforts to gather the value of human resources are lead to nothing.

4.3.5 Efficiency

Moreover, HRA-methods must meet the requirements of efficiency, i.e. the costs caused by the application of HRA-methods must be "inevitable" and proportionate to their expected advantage.

4.4 Stakeholders' Demands

If HRA-methods were implemented in the Hessian state administration, different stakeholder groups would have certain expectations towards it. The most important stakeholder groups would be state executives, employees, tax payers, customers, politics as well as private and public employers.

4.4.1 Executive Managers

Often, Hessian state executives neither know which overall qualifications their employees have, nor do they know whether their employees are employed adequately or rather below or above their qualifications. However, executives should be interested in getting to know the value of their employees to assign them to an area of responsibility corresponding to their qualifications within the scope of their activity field. Thus, they could appreciate their employees better, notably immaterially. As a consequence, an increased employee satisfaction and a more efficient staff employment could lead to more cost-saving work, which in turn would have a positive effect on the performance of the respective part of the authority. This positive performance would again stem from the executive. What is more, executives in the Hessian state administration generally don't know which costs arise from the areas of staff recruitment up to the release of servants. Because of missing cost transparency in all the phases of the value chain of the HR department, this leads to the fact that those costs generally are considered too little – with the effect that costs turn out higher than this would be the case if cost transparency was given.

4.4.2 Employees

Employees in the civil service of Hesse could be interested in having revealed their organizational value, e.g. by the assessment of their qualifications. Thus, they would be more appreciated not only by their superiors, but also in the whole organization. As previously mentioned in point 4.2.2.1 of this work, current employee qualifications often aren't considered on the whole in the civil service; this, however, frequently leads to inefficient employment. Both the disclosure of qualifications and the assessment of human resources by means of Human Resource Accounting methods would contribute to the fact that employments would match better the employees' qualifications; as a consequence, the employees would be more motivated and thus, even work more efficiently.

Qualified and ambitious servants of the land Hesse might be especially interested in having their HR value assessed in the authority they work for: Employees who are open-minded about a continuous further qualification and about vocational education constantly increase their value for the organization by participating in advanced training courses: By doing this, they get the right qualifications for the constantly increasing requirements in the Hessian civil service. From a qualified employee, higher future benefits can be expected by the organization he works for. The measurement of the increased "value" of each individual can thus be used as a selection basis for the group of people considered as suitable for the next promotion round.

In contrast to this, a considerable amount of servants could be suspicious and skeptical about the implementation of HRA-methods in the public service. The reasons for this are the following ones:

1. Servants who are not interested in regularly participating in advanced training courses might fear that their HR value is possibly lower in comparison to the one of their colleagues. Furthermore, they might worry about career-related disadvantages.

2. In order to assess HR values and to make the "internal comparability" of employees possible, it would be necessary to gather and analyze personal-related data in a wider and deeper way than this used to be the case up to now. Because of this, especially if servants disagree with the assessment of their HR value, problems could come up in the field of data protection laws. What is more, in the civil service, the fear of becoming a "transparent employee" could provoke resistance against the use of Human Resource Accounting among unions and staff councils (cf. Gebauer/Wall 2002, 689).

Besides that, the evaluation of HR values provides objective and transparent assessment bases for promotions and for incentive bonuses, as the actual opacity of assessment bases leads to employee demotivation and accordingly, to a drop in performance among a high number of not promoted servants. In all likelihood, the involved costs cannot be compensated by the motivating effect of performance bonuses only to a small number of staff members.

4.4.3 Tax Payers

Tax payers are interested in getting a good, appropriate and realistic overview of existing "assets" or tied funds in the civil service: This goal could be reached by gathering and considering human resource values in accounting. Treating human resources analogously to tangible assets could reveal how efficient human potential is used on the long term. By means of suitable methods of Human Resource Accounting, it could for instance be shown whether the land invests in its workforce to prepare its employees for the increasing requirements in the public sector, or whether staff is rather recruited from outside instead of conducting internal qualification measures; because of recruiting measures, training, reduced employment during the training period and the lack of practical knowledge, the external recruitment would lead to higher costs. Besides, the tax payer could be interested in more efficient decision-making procedures both in the Hessian state politics and administration, brought about by gathering and considering immaterial HR values. Above all, more efficient decisions of public authorities would lead to an improved allocation of public funds - with the effect of a gradual decrease in public debt. As a positive result of this, a lower tax burden could be expected, too.

4.4.4 Customers

Two kinds of clients must be distinguished in the Hessian state administration: internal and external ones. Internal clients are such ones who ask another state authority, another department, a colleague etc. for an internal service. External clients are persons or legal entities putting forward a request from outside an authority, or just persons in a hierarchical relationship with the authority. Participants in internal advanced training courses are an example of internal clients; they are interested in accelerating the corresponding application procedure for internal training courses[27]. This could be managed, for example, by an optimized workflow management, an improved supply of employees with needed facilities, but also by an optimized employee assignment. External trainers for civil servants

---

[27] This desideratum pronounced by Seilheimer (cf. 2007, 72) was meanwhile treated in a project called "Optimierung im Bereich der landesinternen Fortbildung" (Optimization in the area of internal training) initiated on 15th February 2009; this project is finished now, and it has to be awaited which political consequences will be taken out of it or out of further projects.

are an example of external clients. As to the preparation for a seminar, this circle of clients could also be interested in being quickly supplied with seminar information (as the number of participants and their place of work), but also in a quick remuneration payment. The target of internal and external customers is the same one: A rapid handling of their respective matters, which could *ceteris paribus* be reached by an optimized employee assignment.

4.4.5 Politicians

The Hessian Landtag is the state parliament of the land Hesse. It consists of deputies elected by the people (s. 75 par. I Constitution of Hesse, signed on 1st December 1946 (GVBl. p. 229), last amended on 29th April 2011 (GVBl. I p. 182)). For political decision-making, questions put to the Hessian Landtag are often passed on to the competent departments of the state administration to have them answered there. However, data supplied to politics frequently can only be used in a restricted way for decision-making (cf. Brink/Reinemann 2002, 268). As a consequence of this, data graveyards often arise with high efforts, but without being exploitable by politics. Therefore, politicians should be interested in the fact that data provided for decision-making are structured, and assets represented in a realistic way. Particularly in budget questions, it is necessary to get a better overview of "assets" or tied funds in the public service. In the sector of human resources, this could be realized by suitable methods of Human Resource Accounting. The resulting immaterial values could then be used for decision-making, and finally also be taken into account as a basis for economic decisions. This approach would contribute to make Hesse's new borrowings decrease, which in turn would have positive effects on the absolute number of public debt.

4.4.6 Employers

For employers, it is useful to have information on the cost, value and benefits of "their" human resources. This way, they can better appreciate employee values and assign them to jobs answering their skills, competences and talents. As a consequence of this, employers would save costs. Besides, an employer could have an interest in assessing an employee's future contributions to the "success" of the public institution[28]. What is more, it would probably be interesting to know which factors are crucial for better work results.

As the value of human resources is not recorded in the civil service at the moment, we have no overview of the "assets" in Hesse's state administration – except for tangibles shown in accounting up to now. Suitable methods of Human Resource Accounting could contribute to establish cost transparency in the HR sector as well as to support a more realistic and complete presentation of public "assets".

4.5 The Gap between Demand and Reality regarding Human Resource Accounting in Hesse's State Administration

A comparison of the demands and the current situation regarding the use of Human Resource Accounting methods in the Hessian state administration reveals that there are big differences between demand and reality: Up to now, HRA-methods are not applied in the Hessian state administration. In the whole value chain of the HR sector, there is no cost transparency. Labor employment depends on the highest vocational qualification at the beginning of the public employment, and further qualifications usually are not taken into account. After all, servants neither are considered nor treated as valuable assets; therefore, assets are not recorded completely in accounting and, as a consequence, cannot be used as a basis for decision-making in politics and administration. There are no quantitative, objective assessment foundations for promotions and for incentive bonuses.

All those mentioned shortfalls in the accounting system of the HR sector lead to inefficient work in the civil service. They impede a systematic reduction of overall spending and therefore hamper a decrease of the high public debt level.

---

[28] This, however, depends on the area of work, and on how "success" is defined.

5. Suitable Methods of Human Resource Accounting in the Public Service

In the previous chapter, the current deficit situation regarding Human Resource Accounting in the Hessian state administration was the focal point of interest. In this chapter, it will be examined which HRA-methods would be suitable for solving the previously mentioned deficiencies in the civil service.

In scientific discussions, Human Resource Accounting has meanwhile both become practically irrelevant and insignificant as a holistic valuation concept. However, in a sense, it has been replaced by partial and target-specific assessment methods. Therefore, the goal of an HR assessment must be made clear before each application of Human Resource Accounting methods. Without taking into account the aim of a planned assessment, universally valid statements on the profitability of single methods are not possible.

For the civil service, the main targets of HRA-methods can be derived from the gap between the current requirements and the given situation concerning HRA methods in the Hessian state administration (cf. point 4.5 of this work):

1.	The establishment of cost transparency for the whole value chain of the HR sector (i.e. this means from staff recruitment to retirement) by attributing costs to persons (cost bearers)
2.	The establishment of transparency of qualifications for an optimal allocation of employees (within the framework of service law)
3.	The establishment of quantitative, objective assessment bases for promotions and for the grant of incentive bonuses
4.	Improved illustration of assets or tied funds as a basis for decision-making for politics and administration
5.	Creation of a philosophy to consider and treat public employees as valuable resources

Illustr. 15: Main targets of an HRA-system in the civil service

Depending on the requirements of practical work in the public administration, even more targets are possible. In the following, it will be analyzed to which extent each HRA-method can reach the above-mentioned targets.

5.1 Historical Cost Method

The method of historical acquisition costs or rather the cost value method is worth being considered for application in the civil service: Its aim would be an improved illustration of assets or tied funds in accounting. A secondary aim would be the creation of cost transparency in the whole value chain in the HR sector as well as the creation of transparency of employee qualifications. The method of historical acquisition costs is suitable for a transfer to the civil service, provided that there are escape clauses in the respective public budget law. According to s. 71a cl. 1 LHO as amended by the Act on 17th December 2007 (GVBl. I p. 908), bookkeeping can be done additionally in accordance with the principles of proper accounting and balancing in conformity with the general accounting principles of the German Commercial Code ("Handelsgesetzbuch") (HGB) in the Hessian civil service. The first time to make use of these provisions was in 2009; one year later, in 2010, the Hessian Treasury Secretary, Dr. Thomas Schäfer, presented a state-specific overall annual statement according to the principles of the German Commercial Code (cf. HMdF 2012, 1). The Commercial Code was applied analogously and in a restricted way for Hessian state accounting. According to s. 253 I, II HGB, assets may be recorded at the utmost with their acquisition or manufacturing costs, which must be cut obligatorily by depreciations set forth by s. 253 II, III HGB. The application of the historical acquisition cost method in companies with relatively highly qualified employees shows that its use in auxiliary calculations can be of prime importance – in particular with regard to personnel decisions (cf. Schoenfeld 1974, 23).

In order to make the calculation of individual human assets possible, investment accounts have to be created first by means of suitable software before applying the cost value method in the civil service and before showing human assets in the balance sheet.

investment account of Chief Secretary Dr. Meyer			
Acquirement	20.000	Depreciation, further	
Training	15.000	education (5 years)	5.000
Further education	25.000	Depreciations, Expenditures on acquisitions (10 years)	3.500
		Final inventory	51.500
	60.000		60.000

Tab. 10: Individual investment account (cost value method)

Subsequently, human assets are integrated in the profit and loss account as follows (cf. Schoenfeld 1974, 21-23):

conventional yields(in €)				10,000,-
conventional expenditures (in €)			60,000,-	
%	*investments in human resources*			
	new engagements	40,000,-		
	increase due to personnel transfer	15,000,-		
	employees' knowledge preservation			
	and improvement	30,000,-	85,000,-	
			145,000,-	
-	*decrease in value of human resources*			
	dismissals	5,000,-		
	losses owing to staff transfer	10,000,-		
	obsolescence of knowledge	25,000,-		
	health effects	8,000,-		
	depreciation	20,000,-	68,000,-	77,000,-
annual earnings /annual loss				67,000,-

Tab. 11: Example of an HR profit and loss statement (cost value method) in the public sector

In a further step, all individual HR values are accumulated to finally show the overall HR value in the balance sheet. This looks like as follows (cf. Beyer 1991, 163):

balance sheet			
fixed assets	...	equity capital	...
current assets	...	outside capital	...
human assets	...	human capital	...

Tab. 12: Human assets in the balance sheet – method of historical costs

In the *balance sheet*, the HR value is represented on the asset side to which a corresponding debit item of the same amount is opposed on the liabilities side. The assignment to equity capital or borrowed capital depends on the asset concept (cf. Schoenfeld 1974, 21). The question of property can be avoided by showing the debit item including human assets separately.

The use of the cost value method in the civil service includes the following advantages and disadvantages:

Advantages	Disadvantages
• analogous treatment of immaterial human assets and tangible assets in accounting • relatively simple traceability of the HR assessment • The method appears to be suitable for its practical use in the civil service. • Calculated human resource values can support politics and executives in taking more efficient decisions. • Better appreciation of the quality-oriented HR sector in comparison with other sectors (budgeting etc.)	• Uniform evaluation of human resources is not possible until periods of use or depreciation periods are bindingly given within the scope of assessment rules. • Periods of use and depreciation are estimated values or experience values. • Suitable software is needed for the calculation of HR values. • high expenses for the acquisition of suitable software • increased expenditure due to the collection of additional data

Illustr. 16: Advantages and disadvantages of the cost value method in the civil service

The cost value method meets the requirements of validity and practicability. Furthermore, the method is objective and reliable, provided that both binding periods of use and binding depreciation periods are regulated by assessment rules. All in all, the cost value method is suitable for being practically applied in the public sector.

5.2 Replacement Cost Method

The replacement cost method can be used to calculate HR values on a present value basis. One prerequisite for its application in the civil service is that the replacement costs of employees are known. As this often isn't the case, an approximate replacement cost value has to be found. Such an approximate value results from the capitalization of the employee's original acquisition and training costs at the "desired replacement time".

Example 1:

Mr. Schön has a degree in Business Administration and is engaged in the senior service of a regional board at the time t = 0. The original acquisition and learning costs accounted for € 12.500,-. Now, the replacement value is searched at the time = 6, the rate of price increases amounting to 3%.

$$€ \ 12,500,- \text{ x } (1 + 3\%)^6 = \textbf{€ 14,925.65}$$

Example 2:

Mrs. Klein, superintendent, with a degree in Public Administration, has been working in a regional board for one year. There, she had already been recruited and trained as an aspirant during her training (The training of officers of the non-technical, higher intermediate civil service takes place internally, the corresponding three-year-studies are undertaken at special Universities of applied sciences with a focus on administrative matters). The original acquisition and learning costs accounted for € 75,000,- (€ 4,500,- for the selection procedure, € 70,000,- for both the studies and accompanying internships as well as € 500,- for an introductory seminar after being assigned to a certain post). Now, the replacement value is searched at the time t = 6, considering an accumulating factor of 3%:

$$€ \ 75,000,- \text{ x } (1 + 3\%)^6 = \textbf{€ 89,553.92}$$

If the original costs for the studies and the internships remained unconsidered – this would be the case if the officer could be replaced by another person who finished his or her training at another authority –, Mrs. Klein's resulting replacement value and human resource value would result as follows:

(€ 500,- [introductory seminar] + € 4,500,- [selection procedure]) x (1 + 3%)^6 = € 5,970.26

This example shows the difficulty of applying the replacement cost method in the civil service: Employees with a completely external education (i.e. an education that was not carried out within the public administration) like the members of the higher service without an intern traineeship (for example economists, social scientists, university graduates in public finance), usually have a lower human resource value due to this HRA-method than those people with an - at least - partial internal education (intern traineeship) or a completely internal training. The consequence of this is that members of the higher intermediate service – they get an internal training and often remain in the same authority after their studies – usually have a higher HR value than members of the higher service – they usually have a university or master degree – without an internal education. This "bias of HR values" becomes even more apparent when comparing members of the (previously) lower or middle grade of the civil service in comparison with externally trained members of the higher service. When calculating human resource values on the basis of replacement costs, this problem can only be resolved by always taking for granted external staff recruitment and not considering learning costs within the context of vocational training.

All in all, using the replacement cost method in the civil service implies the following advantages and disadvantages:

Advantages	*Disadvantages*
• facilitating the use of calculated HR values for staff planning and staff recruitment • Calculated HR values can help employers take more efficient staff decisions. • Getting an overview of current employee qualifications • Improved appreciation of employees because of cost transparency • The quantitative assessment of HR values becomes possible. • This method seems to be feasible in the civil service if empirical values on the expected useful life and depreciation periods are given. • Better appreciation of the quality-oriented personnel sector in relation to other sections (budgeting etc.)	• The application is only possible if internal vocational trainings remain unconsidered. • The determination of the accumulation factor is difficult. • Periods of use and depreciation are estimated, or empirical values. • Uniform HR assessment is only possible if periods of use and depreciation periods are bindingly prescribed by rules. • Suitable software is needed for the calculation of HR values. • higher expenses to gather additional data • high expenses for the acquisition of suitable software

Illustr. 17: Advantages and disadvantages of the replacement cost method in the civil service

The method of replacement costs meets the requirements of validity and practicability. Like the cost value method, the replacement cost method can also meet the requirements of objectivity and reliability if standard assessment regulations are broadly introduced. It also seems suitable for the creation of cost transparency in the whole value chain of the HR sector, for the establishment of transparency in the area of employee qualification. Furthermore, the above mentioned method helps set up a philosophy to better appreciate the value of public employees.

5.3 Opportunity Cost Method

In authorities, the opportunity cost method can support a qualification-oriented staff employment and reduce costs caused by miscasts. By means of a more efficient staff employment and an involved increased employee motivation, waste costs decrease; this, in turn, contributes to the reduction of the high public debt level. As already mentioned in point 3.1.3 of this work, one problem of the opportunity cost method resides in its underlying subjectivity and lacking practicability, which make it unsuitable for business views. Therefore, its transfer to the public service is not possible either. Further impediments of its application in the public service are the framework of employment law, according to which salary offers are not permitted, given that the payroll depends on salary or pay scales, respectively on job characteristics. Besides, in the public service, it is hardly practicable to evaluate tangible goods at market-prices or to assess HR values on the basis of actual profit and target profit; however, this would be fundamental to find out the value of human assets on the basis of this method.

All in all, the opportunity cost method neither meets the requirements of the quality criteria nor of practicability. Therefore, it is not suitable for a target-oriented application in the public sector – despite the inherent advantages of this method.

5.4 The Adjusted Discounted Future Wages Model

In the civil service, the adjusted discounted future wages model would be suitable for detecting unexploited human resources and, being used as a basis for the development of strategies, to serve for the efficient utilization of human resources. In the following example, it will be analyzed whether this HR-assessment method could be applied in the public service:

The human resource value of the employee Mary Worthwhile shall be calculated on the basis of the adjusted discounted future wages model. Mrs. Worthwhile works as a secretary in the intermediate service in a Hessian District Office. Her annual compensation is € 24,500,- in the year t = 0. For the years t = 1; t = 2; t = 3; t = 4 und t = 5, the social partners negotiated an annual wage increase of 1.2% p.a. In order to calculate the cash value of Mrs. Worthwhile's annual salaries of the next five years, a discount factor (r) of 6.5% is taken as a basis.

year (t = n)	Annual compensation (in €)	discount factor (r = 6,5%)	Cash value (in €)
0	24,500,-	1	24,500,-
1	24,794,-	0.9390	23,281.57
2	25,091.53	0.8817	22,123.20
3	25,392.63	0.8278	21,020.02
4	25,697.34	0.7773	19,974.54
5	26,005.71	0.7299	18,981.57
		sum (t = 1 up to t = 5)	**105,380.90**

Tab. 13: Cash values of future annual compensations at a discount factor of 6.5%

The efficiency ratio can be calculated by comparing the annual internal efficiency with the average efficiency of the branch or the industry sector (cf. Schoenfeld 1974, 11). Because of the cost covering principle prevailing in the civil service, the problem arises neither to have data on efficiency nor data on average efficiency. In certain, limited areas of the public sector, a modified efficiency ratio can be derived from the amount of realized cost savings per given budget or per given staff expenditures. But other reference values are imaginable for the calculation of an efficiency ratio, too. In order to guarantee a uniform evaluation by using the adjusted discounted future wages model in the civil service, it would be of prime importance to take the same reference values as a basis all over the country. This would probably be the case only if such reference values were fixed in future assessment provisions. The analysis of efficiency ratios could be carried out by means of an annual transmission of authority-related data to a central unit like the Ministry of Finance or the German Federal Statistical Office; there, efficiency key figures of all authorities could be gathered and collated by means of suitable software; this way, average rates could be calculated, too.

The case of Mary Worthwhile is based upon an efficiency ratio of 1.4. Thus, Mrs. Worthwhile's HR value accounts for € 147,533.26 (€ 105,380.90 x 1.4). The surplus value amounts to € 42,152.36 (€ 147,533.26 - € 105,380.90). This "positive surplus value" leads to the conclusion that in the present case, no human resources remain unexploited.

As already mentioned in point 3.1.4.1 of this work, HR values assessed by means of the adjusted discounted future wages model and their informative value are strongly dependent on the respective assessment period.

Thus, the HR value of Mary Worthwhile ceteris paribus only amounts to € 92,994.71in an observation period of three years; the corresponding surplus value only comes to € 26,569.92.

Assessing human assets due to the adjusted discounted future wages model implies the following advantages and disadvantages:

Advantages	Disadvantages
• The detection of unexploited human resources in the organization is possible. • The method can serve as a basis for a more efficient utilization of human resources. • An exact forecast of future levels of remuneration is possible if wage increases are known.	• Suitable software is needed for the calculation of human assets. • High expenditure for the purchase of software. • Human assets strongly depend on the assessment period. • The method is not suitable for recording human assets in the balance sheet. • Employee qualifications remain unconsidered. • Difficult and complex calculation of the efficiency ratio

Illustr. 18: Advantages and disadvantages of the adjusted discounted future wages model in the public service

However, the adjusted discounted future wages model can help pursue cost transparency in the whole value chain of the HR department. Furthermore, it supports the creation of a philosophy to consider and treat employees as worthwhile resources or "assets". Even though it doesn't meet the requirements of objectivity and reliability, this problem could be sorted out if politics established binding assessment rules for the application of this accounting method in the public service.

5.5 Method of Future Earnings

One of the prerequisites to apply the method of future earnings in the civil service is the possibility to assign servants to occupation groups for which age-related income profiles exist. A functional classification of staff groups is the one of public servants, employees, and workers. For these occupation groups, income profiles result from Civil Servants' Remuneration Acts for officers on the one hand, from Collective Agreements for Public Service Employees[29] or from corresponding state Acts for public employees on the other hand; above all, there are general wage agreement contracts or corresponding state Acts for workers from which income profiles can be derived. The projection of future salary or wage increases, however, is difficult. In contrast to this, the calculation of the maximum remaining working time up to retirement age appears to be uncomplicated in the public service. Yet, the determination of a probability factor to weight the remaining working time causes problems. Even if statistical values exist, strongly differing individual probabilities might result. In the following, an example of the method of future earnings is shown for the public sector:

Mrs. Wolf is 57 years old, and works as an officer in the higher intermediate service. She is in the pay group A 13 of the Berlin Senate. The individual HR value of Mrs. Wolf shall be calculated on the basis of the method of future earnings. The calculation takes the following steps:

1. Mrs. Wolf's assignment to the officers of the higher intermediate service, pay group A 13, final level of seniority.
2. Payment profiles can be derived mathematically. The annual salary adjustment of 0.5% is expected for the next 10 years. The present annual earnings amount to € 43,000,-.
3. The remaining time in the authority until retirement by law is 8 years at maximum.
4. The probability factor, taken out of internal statistics, is 0.96. Thus, the weighted working time expectancy is **7.68 years** (8 years x 0.96).
5. The calculation of future earnings can be seen in the payment profile presented in table 14.
6. € 267,334.61 (amount of the discounted remuneration x 0,96 (probability factor of the working time expectancy) = **€ 256,641.22** = **HR value of Mrs. Wolf**

---

[29] This is the "Tarifvertrag für den öffentlichen Dienst (TVöD), issued on 13th September 2005, last amended on 31st March 2012. Formerly, the "Federal Employees Tariff Contract" (Ger. "Bundesangestelltentarifvertrag" cited "BAT"), last amended on 31st January 2003, was in force.

age	Development of earnings	Discount factor i = 6,5%	Cash values for i = 6,5%	accumulated cash values
...				
57	43,000	1	43,000	-
58	43,215	0.9390	40,578.89	40,578.89
59	43,431.08	0.8817	38,293.18	78,872.07
60	43,648.24	0.8278	36,132.01	115,004.08
61	43,866.48	0.7773	34,097.41	149,101.49
62	44,085.81	0.7299	32,178.23	181,279.72
63	44,306.24	0.6853	30,363.07	211,642.79
64	44,527.77	0.6435	28,653.62	240,296.41
65	44,750.41	0.6042	27,038.20	267,334.61

Tab. 14: Payment profile for the individual calculation of cash values (method of future earnings)

If used in the public service, the method of future earnings shows the following advantages and disadvantages:

Advantages	Disadvantages
• simple assignment of employees to employee groups • quite simple calculation of an approximate value for future individual salary payments • The calculated value can be used as a basis for decision making of the staff management, the budget sector and politics.	• The assessment is only possible with the help of suitable software. • high acquisition costs for suitable software • The probability factor is controversial. • subjective discount factor for the whole remaining working period in an authority • Future earnings, especially the ones of public officials, often don't reflect their value for the authority, as their remuneration is a kind of pension ("alimentation"), and not a salary (there is no employment contract). • Expenditures for formation and further education remain unconsidered. • Substandard or above standard employment is not taken into account. • Group-dynamic effects are neglected when adding up individual HR values to the overall HR value. • The possibility of (horizontal or vertical) job changes remains unconsidered

	<ul><li>nonobservance of empirical values: very high HR values of young servants face very low ones of elder servants</li></ul>

Illustr. 19: Advantages and disadvantages of the method of future earnings in the civil service

If there were clear and binding "probability tables", established by politics to support a uniform HR assessment, the above mentioned method would meet the requirements of the quality criteria, and practicability. In such a case, the method would be suitable for being applied in the public service, and to create cost transparency in the whole value chain of the human resources department. Furthermore, it could help establish a philosophy to consider and treat servants as worthwhile "assets".

5.6 The Goodwill Method

The goodwill method is based upon the assumption that business results above branch average can be traced back to an asset which is not recorded on the balance sheet. In order to transfer the goodwill method to the public service for the valuation of human assets, a profit and loss statement as well as of a "branch average" are needed, as the business result "above average" is crucial for the calculation of HR values. As it is not usual to focus on profits in the public service because of the cost covering principle prevailing there, another assessment basis for human resources must be found. For instance, it would make sense to "share" economies in the field of tangible goods by way of "distributing" them among the employees of an organization. What is more, the goodwill method should be used in a broader scope for reasons of practicability. So for an HR assessment by means of the goodwill method, it would be recommendable to consider the different German laender as a branch, and generate an efficiency competition by comparison of the "results" of the German states. Even if only an average value results from the conversion of savings on tangible goods per employee, it becomes apparent if employees work very efficiently because of the economic use of tangible goods in a certain part of an authority. The reason for this is that efficient work or task fulfillment results in the overall decrease in the consumption of tangible goods. The assessment bases of the goodwill method are very objective; however, the method only meet the basic requirements of practicability if it is used extensively in the public sector: A good example of this could be an efficiency competition among the German laender. So by means of the goodwill method, a nationwide efficiency competition could be generated in the public sector – this could finally contribute to cut both expenditures on tangible goods and the high overall expenses of German states. This way, national debt could be reduced soon. The use of the goodwill method includes the following advantages and disadvantages in the public service:

Advantages	Disadvantages
• The method leads to increased responsibility when handling personnel, tangible and financial resources. • The calculated HR values can be used particularly as a basis for decision-making by the budget sector as well as by politics. • making the creation of an efficiency competition among German states possible	• individual HR values remain unconsidered • superior or inferior staff deployment is not taken into account • Expenditures on formation and further education are neglected. • The assessment of HR values is only possible after adopting provisions concerning the HR assessment. • The valuation can only be conducted with the help of suitable software. • high acquisition costs for suitable software

Illustr. 20: Advantages and disadvantages of the goodwill method in the public service

5.7 Method of Contributions to Performance

The Method of contributions to a company's performance exists in two variations: The first one leaves off the consideration of different hierarchy levels, whereas the second one, called "Stochastic Rewards Valuation Model", takes them into account. The basic assumption of both models is that the performance of each employee can be measured in terms of assessable performance contributions to the operational overall performance.

5.7.1 The Method of Future Contributions without Hierarchy Levels

In order to asses public HR values by means of the first alternative of this method, three factors are crucial:

1. the employee's position in an authority
2. the employee's performance level in a certain job
3. the employee's remaining working period in each position.

Additionally, all those three factors are weighted with different possibilities. Whereas the analysis of an employee's "position" in an authority is possible with the aid of the assignment to a career group, to a position, and the involved classification to a salary bracket or fare system, the measurement of the performance level is a problem, as a standardized performance measurement is neither conducted uniformly nor according to objectively defined assessment criteria. Furthermore, the estimation of the remaining working time in the respective positions is not possible, as up to now, career management hardly exists. This makes a prognosis on future positions rather impossible: It cannot be estimated beforehand whether and when employees start active job search or even switch to another hierarchy level. For this reason, the determination of probability factors to weight these three factors with is not possible either. In addition, the definition of individual performance contributions to an authority's overall performance or of a part of an authority hardly seems feasible. Because of the mentioned deficiencies, this HR-assessment approach neither meets the requirements of the quality criteria, nor the ones of practicability, and therefore isn't suitable for being applied in the public service.

5.7.2 Stochastic Rewards Valuation Model

The Stochastic Rewards Valuation Model is the second variant of the above mentioned HR-valuation model, and proceeds from similar premises. However, within the framework of this method, and with regard to the public service, potentially attainable hierarchy levels are additionally indicated for each employee's individual period of employment. As in the public service, career management is rather unusual, it isn't possible to estimate if and when employees ever switch to another hierarchy level. Therefore, the forecast of an employee's future hierarchy levels is not possible. Apart from this, the Stochastic Rewards Valuation Model includes all the deficiencies mentioned in the context of the first alternative of this model. Even if this method has already been used as a prototype in the private sector, the Stochastic Rewards Valuation Model neither meets the requirements of the quality criteria, nor of practicability; therefore, the method is not suitable for its practical application in the civil service.

5.8 The Behavioral Model

The basic assumption of the behavioral model is that the existing, functioning system of relationships in most of the organizations considerably contributes to the performance of the organization (cf. Schoenfeld 1974, 24). However, the difficulty of this theoretically sound approach lies in entirely gathering and defining the scope of the big number of factors contributing to this system. Up to now, it hasn't been possible to collect all variables contributing to the evaluation of human resources; at the present stage of development, this makes a general application of this method impossible in practice.

Although the use of this assessment approach in the public sector would be of interest to reveal and to take profit out of the value of a given social system of relationships in many ways, the behavioral model doesn't meet the requirements of objectivity, reliability, validity, and chiefly not of practicability. Therefore, it is unsuitable for a transfer to the public service. All methods to assess human resources include the following problem according to Bontis et al. (1999, 4):

> All of the models suffer from subjectivity and uncertainty and lack reliability in that the measures cannot be audited with any assurance.

This problem could be resolved by the introduction of valuation rules for human assets in the public sector; thus, the analogous assessment both of human assets and tangible assets, as well as the objective and reliable determination of periods of use, depreciation periods etc. would be made possible.

If there were accountancy rules or valuation rules for the private sector, they could be transferred to the public sector if this was technically possible and if there were no opposing legal objections. For lack of such valuation rules in the private sector, it should be considered to establish separate ones for human resources in the public sector to enable a uniform HR assessment nationwide. This has already been the case in Finland (cf. Frederiksen/Westphalen 1998, 25). There, the Finnish government established a Human Resource Accounting system together with its social partners, and tested it in the public sector, putting the main emphasis on the following main categories (cf. Frederiksen/Westphalen 1998, 25, and Rouhesmaa and Bjurström 1996, chapter 4): numerical and structural development of the factor "personnel", use of working time, staff-related costs, personnel resources and their development, the employees' physical and mental well-being, efficiency and service ability valuation, and rewards systems. The collated data inform about

> how cost-efficiently human resources are managed, so that the organisation [sic] benefits from its human capital as much as possible, how the organisation has taken care of its personnel, so that they have both quantitatively and qualitatively adequate human resources, how the quality of work and working conditions, personnel resources, efficiency and personnel well-being has been taken care of (Frederiksen/Westphalen 1998, 25, and Rouhesmaa and Bjurström 1996, chapter 4).

The HRA-system used in Finnish public organizations can be easily transferred to private institutions (cf. Frederiksen/Westphalen 1998, 25). So taking the example of Finland, HRA-systems in Germany could also be transferred to the private sector if they proved themselves in the public service.

In a nutshell, this chapter's results on characteristics of Human Resource Accounting methods and on their suitability for the civil service are compiled in the following overview:

HRA-method	objectivity	reliability	validity	practicability
Historical cost method (Cost value method)	X*	X*	X	X
Replacement Cost method	X*	X*	X	X
Opportunity Cost method	-	-	-	-
Adjusted discounted future Wages model	X*	X*	X	X
Method of future earnings	X*	X*	X	X
Goodwill method	X	X	X	X1
Method of future contributions to performance (without hierarchy levels)	-	-	-	-
Stochastic Rewards Valuation Model	-	-	-	-
Behavioral model	-	-	-	-

X = requirements entirely met

X* = requirements conditionally met or met when uniform assessment rules are laid down

X1 = requirements only met when used extensively and uniformly

-   = requirements not met

Tab. 15: Fulfilled requirements of HRA models in the public service

Furthermore, in each single case, it must be examined purpose-specifically whether Human Resource Accounting methods meet the requirement of efficiency. For this purpose, it must also be checked in the respective public institution if the costs related to the application of the desired HRA-methods are proportionate to the correspondingly expected benefits.

6. Applying Human Resource Accounting Methods in the Civil Service

In this chapter, the legal framework for the use of Human Resource Accounting methods in the civil service will be presented at first. In a further step, the requirements for their successful application will be worked out. Finally, structural recommendations for a Human Resource Accounting system in the public sector will round this chapter off.

6.1 The Legal Framework

One of the reasons which have led to stagnation of Human Resource Accounting at the beginning of the eighties of the 20th century were normative problems as, for example, legally embedded participation of the staff council as well as regulations of the Federal Data Protection Act.

6.1.1 Provisions regarding the Protection of Personal Data[30]

Before transferring HRA-methods to the public sector, the respective provisions for the protection of personal data have to be taken into account. To implement HRA-methods in German federal state administrations, the data protection regulations of

---

[30] The notion of "Data Protection" came up in the second half of the 20th century, and is not defined nor interpreted uniquely. Depending on the point of view, it is considered as the protection from /against misuse of data processing, the protection of the right of informational self-determination, the protection of personal rights during data processing or privacy protection. Data Protection stands for the idea that basically, every human being can decide for himself or herself, which ones of his or her personal data are made available to someone else at a certain point of time. This way, data protection wants to prevent everyone from being a "see-through man" (W.A. 2012, 1). In the United States of America, data protection is almost not stipulated by law or other regulations. In many cases, the access to private data is socially accepted such as credit screening before the conclusion of an employment contract or before leasing an apartment. Even if there are provisions for certain subareas as the "Children's Online Privacy Protection Act" (COPPA, Ger. "Gesetz zum Schutz der Privatsphäre von Kindern im Internet"), and for health insurance (the "Health Insurance Portability and Accountability Act" (HIPAA)), there is no regulation for handling personal data (W.A. (2012a, 1).

the land are basically important. For instance, s. 34 of the Hessian Data Protection Act (HDSG) stipulates data protection for employment contracts and relationships in authorities and other public institutions of the land, of communities, and of rural districts. According to s. 34 I cl. 1 HDSG, a public employer is only allowed to use the employees' data if this is necessary to begin, maintain or finish an employment; this is also the case if the employment contract is unwound or if internal measures as well as planning, organizational, social and personnel measures shall be conducted or if a legal provision, a wage settlement or service agreement provide this. The application of Human Resource Accounting methods in the civil service has several targets at the same time: The quantitative evaluation of HR values facilitates the work of the personnel management, and improves planning and organizational procedures in the Hessian state administration. What is more, it provides the creation of objective assessment bases for promotions and for incentive bonuses. Hence, multiple prerequisites laid down in s. 34 par. I cl. 1 HDSG are fulfilled at the same time. As a proper application of an HRA-system is only possible by means of a suitable software system, s. 24 V cl. 1 HDSG has to be observed, too. Due to s. 6 HDSG, the agency must at first hand in the directory of procedure to the staff association before the introduction, the application, the change or the amplification of an automatized procedure to process employee data. The corresponding documents must contain a hint that during the "participation procedure" of the staff council, a statement can be demanded from the Hessian data Protection officer. In case there is a data transfer about employees to external persons and positions (i.e. outside the public sector) as it is the case, e.g., when problems occur in pilot projects that only can get resolved together with external experts, then s. 34 II cl. 1 HDSG has to be obeyed as well. According to this, the transfer of employee data to external persons and positions is only permitted if the recipient has a legitimate interest in it, and if the internal workflow requires this, or if the person concerned has consented before.

In general, personal-related data – i.e. data on personal and factual circumstances of a definite or identifiable natural person pursuant to s. 2 I HDSG – may only be collected with the knowledge of the concerned person (s. 12 I cl. 1 HDSG). Furthermore, concerned persons must be informed on this in writing by data-processing controllers who save personal-related data automatically. In this case, the kind of data and the objective as well as the legal basis of the storage must be mentioned (s. 18 I c. 1 HDSG).

As the example of Hesse shows, the respective state Data Protection Acts have to be taken into account both if HRA-methods are to be broadly introduced into the civil service, or even if they are only to be transferred to partial areas of the public sector.

6.1.2 Staff Council Provisions

Before introducing HRA-methods to the civil service, the legal framework concerning staff council provisions has to be examined, too. For instance, if methods of Human Resource Accounting are to be used in a Federal authority, then the regulations of the Federal Employee Representation Law[31] must be observed.

In general, when technical devices to survey the behavior or the performance of employees are introduced or applied (s. 75 III c. 17 BPersVG), the staff council must have a say by concluding council agreements if and when necessary, and in case there is no legal or tariff provision. Depending on the respective HRA-method, gathering the value of human resources by means of suitable software makes drawing conclusions from employees' performance possible[32]. In such a case, the staff council has to consent before the implementation and application of such software. In other cases, each single case must be analyzed as to the calculation of HR values allows an insight into the behavior or performance of employees. Should this be the case, the staff council must get involved before the use of the respective Human Resource Accounting method.

In the Federal administration, when the implementation of HRA-methods is planned, the staff council must consent to the following personnel-related workers',

---

[31] Federal Law on Employee Representation (Ger. 'Bundespersonalvertretungsgesetz', cited BPersVG) issued on 15th March 1974 (BGBl. I p. 693), last amended by section 7 of the Act on 5th February 2009 (BGBl. I p. 160).

[32] This is the case with the method of future contribution to performance (however, this method is not suitable for a practical application in the Civil Service, see point 5.7 of this work).

employees', and officials' matters In order to facilitate the efficient use not only of personnel and material resources, but also of financial resources:

Workers/Employees	Public officials
• Engagement (s. 75 I c. 1 BPersVG) • Assignment to a superior or inferior job; in cases of upgrading or downgrading (s. 75 I c. 2 BPersVG) • Questions on remuneration within an authority, notably the establishment of remuneration principles, the introduction and the use of new remuneration methods and of their changes, the fixing of piece rates, premium rates, and comparable performance-related remuneration including monetary factors (s. 75 III c. 4 BPersVG)* • Selection of Participants for advanced training courses (s. 75 III c. 7 BPersVG)* • Assessment guidelines (s. 75 III c. 9 BPersVG)*	• Engagement (s. 76 I c. 1 BPersVG) • Promotion; assignment to a higher position with a higher remuneration but without a change of the official title; assignment to a function with another official designation in case of changes of the career group or of the whole career (s.76 I c. 2 BPersVG) • Assignment to a higher or lower job (s. 76 I c. 3 BPersVG) • Selection of participants for advanced training courses (s. 76 II c. 1 BPersVG) • Assessment guidelines (s. 76 I c. 3 BPersVG)

*In case there is no legal or tariff regulation, the staff council must get involved in these cases, if and when necessary, by concluding employment agreements (s. 75 III c. 1 BPersVG).

Tab. 16: Facts for staff council participation in introducing an HRA into the public service

If HRA-methods are planned to be introduced into the German states, the corresponding state regulations (Employees Acts) must be observed: According to s. 94 BPersVG, the provisions of ss. 95 to 106 BPersVG are a framework for the legislation of the laender. This means that the state parliaments can specify the rules of the Employees Acts, taking account of ss. 95 to 106 BPersVG. For this reason, it has to be examined which state regulations of the respective Employees Acts must be obeyed before introducing HRA-methods in German state administrations.

6.1.3 Budget Provisions

If public human assets should also be recorded additionally to the usually recorded assets in accounting (for instance, by means of the cost value method), it must be examined beforehand if escape clauses in the respective budget provisions allow the illustration of human assets in accounting.

In the Hessian state administration, bookkeeping can be supplemented by principles of standard accounting practices and balancing, applying *mutatis mutandis* the regulations of Commercial Law[33]. This was first the case in 2009, when the Commercial Code was applied analogously and in a restricted way for Hessian state accounting[34]. If the Commercial Code[35] allows the additional record of human assets (as a supplement to the usual assets) in accounting, this could be done analogously in the Hessian state administration. The assets and debit items listed in s. 266 II and III HGB have to be recorded in the balance sheet layout by large and medium-size corporations. Due to s. 266 II HGB, the assets side contains posts of fixed assets, current assets and deferred items; the fixed assets are divided into immaterial assets, tangible assets, and financial assets, the current assets in stocks of inventory, claims, and other assets, securities, cash balance, Federal Bank balances, cash in banks, and checks as well as deferred items. From the logical

---

[33] See s. 71a cl. 1 Hessian Budget Provisions (LHO) as amended by the Act on 17th December 2007. Further details are regulated by the Ministry of Finance in consultation with the audit office (s. 71a cl. 2 LHO).

[34] Cf. HMdF 2012, 1. Meanwhile, there has been a change in the former Hessian budget provisions: In 2010, the Hessian Treasury Secretary, Dr. Thomas Schäfer, presented an overall annual statement according to the principles of the German Commercial Code (cf. HMdF 2012, 1). According to the Hessian Treasury Secretary, the new balance sheet is worked out according to Commercial Principles, and it gives an overview of the asset situation, the financial situation and the earning position of the land; this way, Hesse's political and economic acts become transparent for everyone. A consequence of this is that the annual asset and profit developments can be observed better than before. This new transparency in public finances became possible by the adjustment of the accounting system towards double-entry bookkeeping within the framework of the New Administrative Management (cf. HMdF 2012, 1).

[35] German Commercial Code [Ger. 'Handelsgesetzbuch', cited HGB], issued on 10th May 1897) (RGBl. p. 219) as last amended by regulation of sec. 2 par. 39 of the Code on 22nd December 2011 (BGBl. I p. 3044). Bayer (cf. 2004, 121) gives a good overview of general activation possibilities for human investments according to HGB, US-GAAP, and IFRS. Here, this comparison is not treated further.

point of view, human assets could most likely be assigned to immaterial assets. However, among the immaterial assets of s. 266 II A I HGB, only concessions, industrial property rights and similar rights and values as well as licenses to such rights and values (s. 266 II A I Nr. 1 HGB), the goodwill (s. 266 II A I Nr. 2 HGB), and payments in advance (s. 266 II A I Nr. 2 HGB) are mentioned. They are defined as "goods" (in the sense of economic benefit or economic usefulness) without and (essential) material substance, i.e. no materiality or tangibility, and unlike financial goods (claims, liabilities etc.), they are not monetary (cf. Haller 1998, 564). Immaterial assets are not a part of the balance sheet layout of s. 266 II HGB, and, as a consequence, must not be recorded in a commercial balance sheet. The main reason for the fact that investments in staff must not be represented as a line item in external annual accounts is that they lack in ability of abstract activation. The latter takes up the individual usability of a good – at least, in German accounting law. The individual usability of a good requires that the good can either be sold as a subject of legal relations or

> [...] durch die Überlassung von Herrschafts- und Nutzungsbefugnissen oder Verfügungsrechten an Dritte Gegenstand des Rechtsverkehrs sein [kann] (Marx 1994, 2382).

The different treatment of immaterial and material assets is inherent in the whole accounting jurisdiction concerning the German Commercial Law, but it is only compulsory to the external annual accounts (cf. Fischer 1999, 30). This means that human assets may only be recorded in the balance sheet if they are not, as it is common, a part of the external annual accounts, but if they are for example used for internal objectives by the staff management.

For the external annual accounts, only a supplementary illustration of human assets is possible in the appendix of the balance sheet to show a company's asset situation as well as the financial and profit situation in a realistic and complete way. For a corresponding application of provisions of the Commercial Law in the Hessian state administration according to s. 71a cl. 1 LHO, this means that human resources may only be recorded in a balance sheet if the balance sheet is only used for internal purposes. If accounting should also be used for external purposes in the Hessian state administration, human assets mustn't be recorded explicitly, but just be illustrated as a supplement in the annex of the balance sheet.

It must not be forgotten that comparisons in the area of human assets are only possible if uniform measurement standards get established for the HR assessment in the civil service. As long as this is not the case, an objective assessment of human capital in authorities is hardly possible, and calculated HR values of different authorities would be neither comparable nor convincing. This is very important for politics, as the government gets a lot of relevant information for decision-making by authorities. Whilst there are no standard assessment rules for human assets in the Hessian civil service, HRA methods can only be applied and used for objectives of the internal HR management as for example staff recruitment. However, in lack of a corresponding regulation in the private sector, it cannot be expected that such a regulation will be introduced in the public service in the foreseeable future.

6.2 Requirements for implementation

For a successful application of Human Resource Accounting methods in the public administration, certain requirements have to be met. For this reason, a phase concept consisting of the following components would be recommendable for the implementation of such an accounting system:

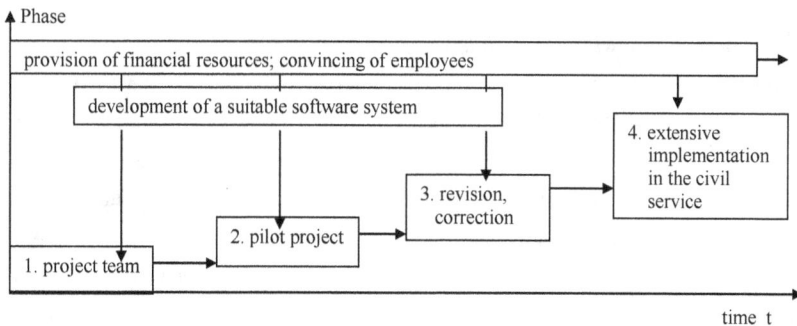

Illustr. 21: Phase concept for the implementation of Human Resource Accounting in the civil service

6.2.1 Convocation of a Project Team

With the support of a fixed-term project team in the first phase of the implementation of HRA-methods in the public service, the elaboration of objectives, the draft of a Human Resource Accounting system for the public service as well as the development of a framework concept for the collection and analysis of reliable information could take place on the basis of already given data. The development of a framework concept in the area of Human Resource Accounting, and the creation of an authority-related Human Resource Accounting system contribute to living up to the respective objectives of authorities. According to Bartscher (cf. 1990, 398), the selection of certain HRA-methods can only take place after finding out the individual organizational objectives of a Human Resource Accounting system. Ideally, this project team comprises motivated employees from the working areas "personnel", "budgeting", and "accountancy"/"controlling", having a business or administrative and/or legal background, and being experienced in administrative work. Should HRA-methods be applied in a broader scope as, for instance, in the whole state administration, the involvement of employees of higher regional boards as project members would be recommendable to stress the political meaning of the project.

6.2.2 The Establishment of a Pilot Project

After the project team has determined the data bases for an HRA-system in the public service, a prototypical test should be conducted in the second step. This way, it can be tested whether HRA-methods meet the respective requirements in practice, and which adjustments are necessary for their application in a wider range of the public service. The pilot project should focus on an important and clearly distinguishable part of the public service like smaller authorities, departments or tightly structured ministry departments. It is neither necessary nor recommendable to apply the whole range of HRA-methods in a pilot project phase, as communication problems and difficulties could come up in case of a radical implementation of HRA-methods (cf. Brummet 1982, 71). Especially in the starting phase of the project, but also during the overall introduction of HRA-methods, the measurement should be kept easy, and there should be a focus on certain areas "if it is clear that such measurements will inform decision making" (Armstrong 2001,

59). Problems occurring during the pilot project phase must be described precisely, and resolved with the help of external experts like computer experts or controllers, if and when necessary. When doing this, the framework of data protection provisions must be observed, too, as described in section 6.1 of this work.

6.2.3 Review and Adjustment of the Original Concept

During the pilot project phase or subsequently to it, the original Human Resource Accounting system must be reviewed, worked over, and adjusted purpose-specifically with regard to occurred problems in practice.

6.2.4 Broad Integration of HRA-Methods into the Public Sector

After this, an introduction of Human Resource Accounting methods can take place all over the country. Following Sailer (cf. 1989, 78), the subsequent strategy would be recommendable for his: During the initial phase, the capacity of Human Resource Accounting can be shown by means of a relatively simple instrument like the replacement cost method, and by data already available for staff-related decision-making processes in the public service. In further stages, an improvement of the data basis and of the quality of decisions can be attained by the cooperation with qualified employees of the line.

6.2.5 Supply of Financial Resources

In all four phases of the implementation process of a Human Resource Accounting system in the public service, it is absolutely necessary to make available financial resources. These ones could either be taken out of the current budget – in terms of reduced expenses for other items –, and/or be financed by higher cash receipts; ideally, there would be a separate item for them in the budget. As the implementation of a Human Resource Accounting system needs a good resource management, and costs can result very high in this phase, an incremental introduction of HRA-methods into the civil service would be recommendable. For this reason, the required financial resources should, as mentioned above, be ideally made available in a separate item of the budget.

6.2.6 Convincing Employees

Moreover, it would be necessary to familiarize public employees with the functions and objectives of a Human Resource Accounting system at an early stage – early before the implementation of a HRA system takes place. In this context, employees should get convinced of the advantages of such a system, because otherwise, fears and resistances could come up against its implementation. Moral objections could be raised, too, if human assets and tangible assets were treated equally ("the equal treatment of humans and machines"). Convincing is most notably important for those public employees who will have the future task to gather and process data for Human Resource Accounting methods. In addition to that, the anticipated effects of HRA-methods on each stakeholder group must be shown beforehand, too. In the public service, convincing can only be realized effectively if Human Resource Accounting methods are implemented in an evolutionary process, with the involvement of employees. Yet, such a process may last for several years.

6.2.7 The Supply of a suitable Software System

The development of a suitable software system for the calculation of HR values is very important in the first three phases of the implementation process of a Human Resource Accounting system in the public service. Earlier attempts to introduce such methods in companies often failed because needed information wasn't available or because the big amount of information couldn't be handled with. Due to the current stage of development of information technology, there are many software programs capable of processing and evaluating complex information; for the establishment of Human Resource Accounting in the public sector, the use of such a suitable software system would be recommendable for the internal administrative context. What is more, when using a networked database system, data gathered once could be used for various purposes; this, in turn, would have time and cost saving effects. Despite the expected high acquisition costs of such a software system, it should be taken into account that the use of HRA-methods would contribute to provide qualitatively better bases for decision-making; furthermore, an improved allocation of personnel, material and financial resources would be possible, too. With regard to the high level of public expenditures, further positive effects would be cost saving effects in the medium term, and the decrease of the high public debt level as well as a positive contribution to the provisions of the debt brake in the long run.

6.3 Structural Recommendations

The integration of a Human Resource Accounting system into the public service depends on a larger number of factors: Thus, the kind, size, and structure of an organization as well as the kind, scope, and quality of existing Human Resource Accounting information (cf. Flamholtz, 1986, 78f) are crucial for the structural organization of an HRA-assessment system in the public sector or in single authorities.

The implementation of a Human Resource Accounting system in organizations is also dependent on the respective institutional size: As a part of the domain of "personnel controlling", different incorporations of such a Human Resource Accounting system are possible (cf. Hentze/Kammel 1993, 203-207):

1. as a staff unit of human resource management or the head of the institution
2. as a line function when the HR department is structured functionally
3. as the head-office department in the main department of personnel or
4. as a part of personnel controlling when personnel management and managerial tasks generally are conducted independently in the line

The workflow management should be organized in such a way that HR values are made available goal-specifically for the stakeholder groups. The nature of how relevant information is provided depends on the respective target group. Relevant management and decision-making information could thus be forwarded to politics as soon as specific questions arise on a certain human resource-related subject in authorities. With the aid of a reporting system, changes in human assets could be shown regularly to the respective heads of authorities. In case of negative trends, this would make an early intervention by countermeasures possible. Once or twice a year, the report on individual HR values to the respective superiors would be recommendable; thus, bosses could get informed on their employees' current qualifications – and appreciate them better. What is more, this would be a good occasion to take suitable measures in the field of further personnel development, or to talk about concrete job changes. Apart from this, each employee should have the chance to get informed on his or her personal HR value. This could be put into practice by means of intranet or a personal access authorization to another database that stores HR values. This way, each organizational member would also have the opportunity to get informed on personal deficits, and hence, to initiate appropriate countermeasures. Beyond that, in order to inform tax payers on existing assets or tied funds in the public service, the calculated overall HR values should be made available to the public. The ideal means for this would be an auxiliary calculation in the annex of a balance sheet or the income statement. This in turn would give a more complete picture for the accounts, and could, for instance, be realized on internet pages of authorities, provided that the calculated values don't allow drawing conclusions about single employees, and that no personal-related data are disobeyed.

7. Closing Remarks

In this work, various operational in- and output-oriented methods of Human Resource Accounting were presented and illustrated with regard to their application in the civil service: For this purpose, both the notions of "human resources" and "Human Resource Accounting" were defined, and the origins and the distribution of Human Resource Accounting were highlighted at first. In a second step, the general presentation of different Human Resource Accounting methods took place, before the current situation in the civil service of Hesse and the special requirements for a Human Resource Accounting system in Hesse were the focal points of interest. From this, the main objectives of a Human Resource Accounting system could be derived for the civil service. In a further step, it was analyzed in detail which Human Resource Accounting methods would be suitable for a purpose-specific use in the public service. Subsequently, after explaining the legal framework for a Human Resource Accounting system in the civil service, the respective prerequisites for this were outlined. Finally, structural recommendations on the implementation of a Human Resource Accounting system in the civil service round this work off.

To sum it up, the cost value method, the method of replacement costs, the adjusted discounted future wages model, and the method of future earnings would prove themselves suitable for the public sector, provided that not only subjective parameters are eliminated or turned objective and reliable, but also that databases are adapted to special requirements, and standard assessment provisions get established. Even without standard assessment rules for human resources in the public sector, the application of Human Resource Accounting methods in single authorities would contribute to pave the way for cost transparency in the civil service; however, comparisons between different authorities or even between different federal states would only be possible after the widespread and standardized use of such methods. In Hesse, the partial use of such methods could perhaps be put into practice in projects subsequent to the already terminated one "Optimierung im Bereich der landesinternen Fortbildung" (Optimization in the area of internal training). It has now to be awaited which political consequences will be taken out of it or out of further projects. All in all, the application of Human

Resource Accounting methods in the public sector would not only lead to the reduction of inefficient decision-making, but also to the decrease both in public overall expenditures and in the high level of public debt. This way, it would also be a good contribution to keep the conditions of the debt brake to renounce new borrowings at the end of this decade. To this end, it would be desirable if this book was not only registered – and perhaps further developed – by academics, but also by open-minded members of the civil service and in politics.

V. Bibliography

Armstrong, M. (2001): A Handbook of Human Resource Management Practice, 8th ed., 57-60.

Aschoff, C. (1978): Betriebliches Humanvermögen - Grundlagen einer Humanvermögensrechnung. Wiesbaden.

Bartscher, Th.R./Steinmann, O. (1990): Der Human-Resource-Accounting-Ansatz innerhalb der Personal-Controlling-Diskussion, in: Zeitschrift für Personalforschung, N°. 4, 387-401.

Basic Law for the Federal Republic of Germany [Ger. 'Grundgesetz', cited GG] (1949), first issue of the *Federal Law Gazette*, dated 23rd May 1949, as amended up to and including 21st July 2010 I 944.

Bayer, K. (2004): Investitionen in Humanvermögen: Entwicklung von Bilanzierungsregeln für den informationsorientierten Jahresabschluss. Hamburg: Kovac, 2004. Schriftenreihe zum betrieblichen Rechnungswesen und Controlling; 17. Zugleich: Münster (Westfalen), Univ., Diss., 2003.

Beyer, H.-T. (1991): Personallexikon, 2nd ed., München/ Wien, 57-60.

Bontis, N./Dragonetti, N./Jacobsen, K./Roos, G. (1999): The Knowledge Toolbox: A review of the tools available to measure and manage intangible resources. European Management Journal. N°. 17, 4, 391-402; also on http://www.business.mcmaster.ca/mktg/nbontis/ic/publications/BontisEMJ.pdf, last called 22nd August 2012, 1-19.

Bösch, R.E. (1979): Möglichkeiten der Berücksichtigung des Humanvermögens bei der Unternehmensbewertung. Diss. University of St. Gallen. St. Gallen, 20ff.

Brink, St./ Reinemann, H. (2002): Parlamente im Prozess der Verwaltungsmodernisierung, in: Verwaltung & Management, 265- 272.

Brummet, R.L. (1982): Die Erfassung des Humankapitals in Unternehmen – Ziele, Aufgaben, Bedeutung, in: Schmidt, H. (Hrsg.): Humanvermögensrechnung – Instrumentarium zur Ergänzung der unternehmerischen Rechnungslegung: Konzepte und Erfahrungen. Berlin/New York, 61-72.

Brummet, R.L./Flamholtz, E.G./Pyle, C.P. (1968): Accounting for Human Resources, in: Michigan Business Review, Vol. 20, N°. 2, 20-25.

Burth, A. (2011): Verschuldung in Hessen. Landesverschuldung. www.haushaltssteuerung.de/verschuldung-land-hessen.html (22nd October 2011), called 1st August 2012.

Civil Servants' Remuneration Act (Ger. 'Bundesbesoldungsgesetz', cited BBesG) consolidated version issued on 19th June 2009 (BGBl. I p. 1434), last amended by section 7 of the Act on 21st July 2012 (BGBl. I p. 1583).

Collective Agreements for Public Service Employees (Ger. 'Tarifvertrag für den öffentlichen Dienst', cited 'TVöD', issued on 13th September 2005, last amended on 31st March 2012.

Conrads, M. /Goetzke, W. /Sieben, G. (1982): Human Resource Accounting: Entscheidungs-rechnung über das betriebliche Humanvermögen; Schmidt, H. (ed.): Humanvermögensrechnung – Instrumentarium zur Ergänzung der unternehmerischen Rechnungslegung: Konzepte und Erfahrungen. Berlin/New York, 493-502.

Constitution of Hesse (Ger. 'Verfassung des Landes Hessen'), signed on 1st Dezember 1946 (GVBl. p. 229), last amended by the Act on 29th April 2011 (GVBl. I p. 182).

Dawson, C. (1988): The Accounting Approach to Employee Resourcing, in: Management Decision 5, 31-36.

Deutsch, R. (1997): Nach traditionellen Bewertungsmethoden sind Aktien derzeit extrem überbewertet (U.S.A.), http://www.gold-eagle.com/analysis/stocks_over-valued_german.html, last called 15th August 2012.

Eichenberger, P. (1992): Betriebliche Bildungsarbeit. Return on Investment und Erfolgs-controlling, Wiesbaden.

Federal Employees Tariff Contract (Ger. 'Bundesangestelltentarifvertrag', cited 'BAT'), last amended on 31st January 2003.

Federal Law on Employee Representation [Ger. 'Bundespersonalvertretungsgesetz', cited BPersVG) issued on 15th March 1974 (BGBl. I p. 693), last amended by section 7 of the Act on 5th February 2009 (BGBl. I p. 160).

Fischer, H. (1999): Zur Erfassbarkeit von Personalinvestitionen im internen Rechnungswesen; in: Zeitschrift für Personalforschung 13(1), 29-66.

Fischer-Winkelmann, W.F./Hohl, E.K. (1982): Konzepte und Probleme der Humanvermögensrechnung, in: Der Betrieb, N°. 51/52, 2636-2644.

Flamholtz, E.G. (1971): A Model for Human Resource Valuation; A Stochastic Process with Service Rewards, in: The Accounting Review, 253-267.

Flamholtz, E.G. (1974): Human Resource Accounting, London/San Francisco.

Flamholtz, E. G. (1986): Which HR-Accounting System Fits Your Organization, in: Personnel Journal, 75-81.

Frederiksen, J.V./Westphalen, S.-A. (1998): Human Resource Accounting: interests and conflicts. A discussion paper, in: CEDEFOP, European Centre for the Development of Vocational Training, N°. 3, Thessaloniki.

Frese, Yorck (2012): Staatsverschuldung in Deutschland nach der Föderalismusreform II – eine Zwischenbilanz", in: Deutsches Verwaltungsblatt DVBl. N°. 3, 1st February 2012, 127th year, 153-156.

Gabler Wirtschaftslexikon (1993), 13th ed., Wiesbaden.

Gebauer, M./Wall, F. (2002): Human Resource Accounting zur Unterstützung der Unternehmensrechnung, in: Controlling: Zeitschrift für erfolgsorientierte Unternehmens-steuerung, 685-690.

Gebauer, M. (2002): Human Resource Accounting, Measuring the Value of Human assets and the Need for Information Management; in: Badovinac, B. et al. (ed.): Human Beings and Information Specialists, Proceedings. Ljubliana, Stuttgart, 80-89.

Gerpott, T. J. (1990): Erfolgswirkungen von Personalauswahlverfahren: Zur Bestimmung de ökonomischen Nutzens von Auswahlverfahren als Instrument des Personal-Controlling, in: Zeitschrift für Führung + Organisation, 59th year, 37-44.

Haller, A. (1998): Immaterielle Vermögenswerte – Wesentliche Herausforderung für die Zukunft der Unternehmensrechnung, in: Möller/ Schmidt (ed.): Rechnungswesen als Instrument für Führungsentscheidungen. Festschrift für A.G. Coenenberg. Stuttgart 1998, 561-596.

Hamel, W. (1987): Personal als Investition, in: Schmalenbachs Zeitschrift für betriebswirtschaftliche Forschung, 39th year, 1079-1087.

German Commercial Code [Ger. 'Handelsgesetzbuch', cited HGB] (1897) (RGBl. p. 219) as last amended by regulation of sec. 2 par. 39 of the Code on 22nd December 2011 (BGBl. I p. 3044).

Hekimian, J.S./ Jones C.H. (1967): Put People on Your Balance Sheet, in: Harvard Business Review, Vol. 45, 105-113.

Hentze, J./ Kammel, A. (1993): Personalcontrolling. Eine Einführung in Grundlagen, Aufga-benstellungen, Instrumente und Organisation des Controlling in der Personalwirtschaft. Bern/ Stuttgart/ Wien.

Hermanson, R.H. (1964): Accounting for Human Assets. Occasional Paper N°. 14, East Lansing, Michigan Bureau of Business and Economic Research, Michigan State University.

Hessian Budget Provisions [Ger. 'Hessische Landeshaushaltsordnung', cited LHO] (issued on 15th March 1999 (GVBl. I p. 248), last amended by the Act on 17th December 2007 (GVBl. I p. 908).

Hessisches Ministerium der Finanzen (cited 'HMdF') (2012): Haushaltsplan des Landes Hessen. http://www.hmdf.hessen.de/irj/go/km/docs/Hessen/HMdF/Applikationen/Gesamtha ushaltsplaene/Gesamtplan%202012.pdf, (4th July 2012) Wiesbaden.

Hessisches Ministerium der Finanzen (2003): Schuldenstände in Hessen (1993-2002). Wiesbaden.

Hessisches Statistisches Landesamt (2012): Schuldenstand und Pro-Kopf-Verschuldung des Landes Hessen 2000 bis 2009. http://www.statistik-hessen.de/themenauswahl/finanzen-personal-steuern/landesdaten/finanzen-personal/land/schuldenstand-und-pro-kopf-verschuldung-des-landes-hessen/index.html, 4th July 2012, Wiesbaden.

Hessisches Statistisches Landesamt (2012a): Data on debt levels, debts per inhabitant and new borrowings in 2010 and 2011. Interview 23rd August 2012.

Hessische Staatskanzlei (2012): Jahresabschluss 2010: Hessen ist auf dem Weg. http://www.hmdf.hessen.de/irj/HMdF_Internet?cid=5f3643767551615eb63abf97a8 51da8b, 4th July 2012, Wiesbaden.

Kontner, P. (1980): Humanvermögensrechnung: Untersuchung zu einem personalwirtschaftlichen Führungsinstrument, in: Müller, U./Hundsnurscher, F./Janß, K. W. (ed.), in: Göppinger akademische Beiträge; N°. 111.

Laddo, Ashish N. et al. (2011): Models for measuring HUMAN ASSETS. www.scribd.com/doc/54931164/HRA-various-methods, (5th August 2011), called on 31st July 2012).

Lev, B./ Schwartz, A. (1971): On the Use of The Economic Concept of Human Capital in Financial Statements, in: The Accounting Review, 103-112.

Likert, R./ Bowers, D.G. (1973): Improving the Accuracy of P/L Reporting by Estimating the Change in Dollar Value of the Human Organization, in: Michigan Business Review, Vol. XXV, N°. 2, 15-24.

Maier, F. (1980): Bilanzierung von betrieblichem Humankapital; discussion papers; Internationales Institut für Management und Verwaltung, Berlin.

Marr, R. (1982): Humanvermögensrechnung oder Personalindikatorensysteme? – Die Ermittlung von Informationen über den Wert des Humanvermögens von Organisationen mit Hilfe einer innerbetrieblichen Meinungsforschung, in: Schmidt, H. (Hrsg.): Humanvermögensrechnung – Instrumentarium der unternehmerischen Rechnungslegung: Konzepte und Erfahrungen. Berlin/New York, 549-576.

Marquès, E. (1982): Europäische Erfahrungen bei der Einführung der Humanvermögensrechnung, in: Schmidt, H. (ed.): Humanvermögensrechnung – Instrumentarium zur Ergänzung der unternehmerischen Rechnungslegung: Konzepte und Erfahrungen. Berlin/New York, 227-237.

Marx, F.-J. (1994): Objektivierungserfordernisse bei der Bilanzierung immaterieller Anlagewerte. In: Betriebs-Berater, Berlin/New York, 2379-2388.

Mincer, J. (1962): On-The-Job-Training: Costs, Returns, and some Implications, in: The Journal of Political Economy, Vol. 70, N°. 4, Part 2, 50ff.

Neubauer, F.F. (1974): Neuere Entwicklungen im amerikanischen Rechnungswesen: Das Human Resource Accounting, in: Die Unternehmung; 28th year, 261 ff.

Nicklisch, H. (1932): Die Betriebswirtschaft, 7th ed., Stuttgart.

OECD (1996): Measuring What People Know. Paris.

Paton, W.A. (1922): Accounting Theory, New York, 486.

Philips, J. (1996): Accountability in Human Resource Management. Houston: Gulf Publishing Company.

Pyle, W.C. (w.y.): Development of A Human Resource Accounting Model, in: Brummet et al., 23-30.

Rouhesmaa, H./ Bjurström, L.M. (1996): Human Resource Accounting in Finnish Enterprises, working paper presented at the seminar on Human Resource Accounting in Enterprises: Recent Practices and New Developments, co-hosted by the Finnish Ministry of Labour and OECD, Helsinki, 19-20th March 1996.

Sackmann, S.A. (1989): Human resource accounting: State-of-the-art-review, in: Journal of Accounting Literature, 235-264.

Schoenfeld, H.-M. (1974): Die Rechnungslegung über das betriebliche Humanvermögen, in: Betriebswirtschaftliche Forschung und Praxis, N°. 1, 1-32.

Schultz, T.W. (1971): Investment in Human Capital, in: American Economic Review, Vol. 51, 1-17.

Seiler, M. (1989): Personal-Controlling. Ein Instrument zur strategischen Entwicklung und ökonomischen Fundierung der Personalarbeit, I.FPM-Forschungspapier, St. Gallen.

Seilheimer, A. (2007): Die Humanvermögensrechnung. Geeignete Verfahren des Human Resource Accounting im öffentlichen Dienst. Stuttgart: Ibidem.

Sekretariat des Stabilitätsrates (2012): Konsolidierungshilfengesetz. http://www.stabilitaetsrat.de/DE/Organisation/Gesetzliche-Grundlagen/Konsolidierungshilfengesetz/Konsolidierungshilfengesetz_node.html (last called on 13th August 2012).

Sprouse, T., und Moonitz, M. (1962): A Tentative Set of Broad Accounting Principles for Business Enterprises, AICPA, New York, 2.

Streim, H. (1982): Fluktuationskosten und ihre Ermittlung, in: Schmalenbachs Zeitschrift für betriebswirtschaftliche Forschung, 34th year, 128-146.

Streim, H. (1993): Humanvermögensrechnung, in: Kern, Werner u.a. (Hrsg.): Handwörterbuch der Betriebswirtschaft, 5th ed., 1st Vol., Stuttgart, 1681-1694.

Szyperski, N. (1962): Zur Problematik der quantitativen Terminologie in der Betriebswirtschaftslehre, Berlin.

W.A. (2012): Datenschutz. http://de.wikipedia.org/wiki/Datenschutz, (9th July 2012), 1.

W.A. (2012a): Datenschutz. Vereinigte Staaten. http://de.wikipedia.org/wiki/Datenschutz#Vereinigte_Staaten, (9th July 2012), 1.

Winckler, B. (1991): Investitions- und kontrolltheoretische Ansätze der Kostenrechnung. Wiesbaden.

Witte, E. (1962): Forschung, Werbung und Ausbildung als Investitionen, in: Ortlieb, H.-D. (Hrsg.): Hamburger Jahrbuch für Wirtschafts- und Gesellschaftspolitik (7th year), Tübingen, 210-225.

Woods, E.A., und Metzger, C.B. (1927): America's Human Wealth, The Money Value of Human Life. New York, 64.

ibidem-Verlag

Melchiorstr. 15

D-70439 Stuttgart

info@ibidem-verlag.de

www.ibidem-verlag.de
www.ibidem.eu
www.edition-noema.de
www.autorenbetreuung.de

www.ingramcontent.com/pod-product-compliance
Lightning Source LLC
Chambersburg PA
CBHW050537270326
41926CB00015B/3276